PRACTICAL SUGGESTIONS FOR TEACHING

Edited by Alice Miel

————◆————

READING IMPROVEMENT IN THE JUNIOR HIGH SCHOOL

Practical Suggestions for Teaching

TITLES IN THIS SERIES

Reading Improvement

in the

Junior High School

DEBORAH ELKINS

ASSOCIATE PROFESSOR, QUEENS COLLEGE

CITY UNIVERSITY OF NEW YORK

with the assistance of

THELMA HICKERSON

and GEORGE KRIEGER

ASSISTANTS TO THE PRINCIPAL

CAMPBELL JUNIOR HIGH SCHOOL

TEACHERS COLLEGE PRESS

Teachers College, Columbia University

New York

PRINTED IN THE UNITED STATES OF AMERICA

Editor's Foreword

THIS IS A SUCCESS STORY. IT TRACES THE SLOW AND CAREFUL STEPS TAKEN in helping nearly one hundred junior high school girls and boys lose their fear of being stupid. It shows them making a new beginning in reading, an activity with which so much failure had been associated in their previous schooling. In preparing this detailed and colorful account, Dr. Elkins of Queens College and the two administrators, who were closely involved in the reading project, have rendered a great favor to other teachers of adolescents. While describing faithfully the procedures and materials used in the experiment, the author has been careful to show the principles on which the teachers were working and to suggest ways in which other teachers might adapt the general ideas to their own uses.

By the time the reader reaches the end of the story, he will be impressed with the importance of (1) an opportunity for one teacher to work closely with the same group of children for a large block of time each day for more than one year, (2) a combination of total class, small group, and individualized instruction, all under the management of this one teacher working in partnership with the children, (3) an integrated approach through writing, discussing, listening while others read, reading to others, and reading on one's own, (4) an understanding on the part of each child of how one learns to read and evidence that he is making progress, and (5) a focus on content that is meaningful to the particular children being taught. A special point is made of the fact that teaching phonics—or any other skill divorced from meaningful content—can be expected to result only in the reading failure previously experienced by these children.

The entire booklet is packed with good suggestions for teaching but the perceptive teacher will note that there is much more involved than a few appealing ideas for interesting children in reading. A matter of self-respect based on growing competence is at stake and this requires an all-out, consistent, and painstaking effort. That the rewards are continuous and worth the effort is quite evident throughout the text.

ALICE MIEL

Acknowledgments

TO ACKNOWLEDGE ALL THOSE WHO CONTRIBUTED HEAD, HEART, AND HAND to the accomplishment of the many activities that went into the gathering of material and the writing of this pamphlet would be impossible in the short space available here. It has been the happy experience of the author and the administrators to work with many young and interested teachers. We wish to thank at least two of them: Miss Elinor Weinreich, who worked diligently for two full years in this project, and whose efforts in bringing about a desire to do and a feeling of self-worth in children played an important part in carrying the work through successfully; and Mr. Eli Seifman who entered into the study too late for his class to be included here, but who helped in the collection of needed data.

The author is deeply indebted to Mr. Paul Balser, at that time the Principal of Campbell Junior High School 218, who made it possible to work in the school situation described here; to Dr. Joseph O. Loretan, Associate Superintendent of the Junior High School Division of the Board of Education of the City of New York, whose interest in exploring new approaches to junior high school problems has been an inspiration; to Dr. Harry N. Rivlin, Dean, Division of Teacher Education of the City University of New York, who had the vision to see the educational possibilities in developing a close relationship between the Education Department of Queens College and the public school; to Dr. John L. Ames, Director of Teacher Education at Queens College, whose encouragement and demonstration of faith in the endeavor helped this entire project to become a reality; to Dr. Helen Storen, coordinator of the activities that went on between the college and the public school, who lent her continuous support as well as her numerous abilities to keeping doors open to enable people to work; and to Dr. Albert J. Harris, Director of the Education Clinic at Queens College, from whose keen and intelligent criticism of the manuscript, and perceptive suggestions, the author benefited.

Contents

Reading Improvement in the Junior High School

1 • Introduction

"I WAS READING TO MY LITTLE BROTHER AND STOPPED IN THE MIDDLE TO ask him questions and he said, 'Shut up, Andy, and finish reading the story.' He wouldn't let me ask any more questions." The seventh-grade class members were describing their "unusual experiences" encountered while reading to younger siblings or neighbors' children. It was a serious session carried out in the interests of a serious project: to prepare and "publish" well before the Christmas season a list of appropriate books to be used as a buying guide for parents of preschool children.

This was only one of the reading activities planned by the seventh-grade teachers of a large junior high school in a predominantly middle-class residential area[1] of the city of New York. Out of a total of twenty seventh-grade classes there were three groups in which the children were

[1] The community is a residential area in the sense that no industry exists there. Shops such as grocery stores, supermarkets, small hardware and toy shops, and beauty shops serve the daily needs of the people. There are four major types of houses in the area: large "projects," large two-story garden apartments, small attached houses, and single houses. Those in the public housing project have limited incomes which must not be surpassed on pain of jeopardizing the right to live there. Calling this a middle-income neighborhood puts a strain on definition since the income range is great. The other extreme live in single homes with well-tended grounds, homes representing incomes probably much larger than in the public housing project apartments, and many of the single houses are postwar structures. In other words, this is a community which has mushroomed in recent years, with the exception of one section of frame houses built close together with little land in between.

Most of the children in the school are white. The predominant ethnic-religious groups are Jewish and Catholic, the latter largely Italian. About one-third of the families speak another language in addition to English in the home. The fathers' occupations range from lumberyard handyman to doctor. Most are salaried as distinct from wage earners on an hourly or piece basis, although there is a substantial number in this category, too. The majority of the families have only one wage earner, the mother caring for the home and children since the families are young ones. Eighty-six per cent of the parents have had at least some high school education. This description is paraphrased from a study of this community by Dr. Robert Edgar of Queens College and his students.)

1

about two years or more below grade in reading. It is with these three groups of children and their teachers that this pamphlet is concerned. There were 30 children in each group ranging in age on entering from 11 years 9 months to 14 years, and in IQ, as measured in October of the sixth grade, from 67 to 108 with a median IQ of 82. In each of these three classes of 30, eight children had been held over at least one year in the elementary school, and an additional six were serving their second year in the seventh grade. This means that 14 out of every 30 children were repeaters somewhere along the line. The usual reason for retaining a child was lack of achievement in reading. The experience of repeating earlier grades apparently had not helped these children reach grade level.

The teachers who were attempting to guide each of the groups of 30 young people, admittedly large groups considering the fact that the children were seriously below grade in reading, were young and inexperienced. None had had specialized training as reading teachers. Yet they met with an amazing degree of success in helping the children to learn to read. The teachers chosen for the project were those who had the greatest amount of time scheduled to work with the children. They were not handpicked for any other reason. They were the core teachers in charge of English, social studies, and group guidance. They were responsible for the children's learning for thirteen periods per week arranged usually in five double or block periods and three single ones. This meant a total of thirteen 45-minute periods assigned to core.

A consultant from nearby Queens College at first worked with each teacher individually in weekly 45-minute conferences. Later, to save consultant time, she worked with the group of three teachers in such a way that they would learn to help and support each other with a minimum of outside assistance or of administrative aid. The classrooms were visited as often as possible by administrators and by the consultant.

No attempt was made to carry through a controlled piece of research; rather what was sought was an answer to whether children in large numbers could be helped to learn to read, and whether the teachers' ability to do this could be developed with a measure of satisfaction to themselves. There was more concern with what was happening to teachers and children as they made all-out attempts to solve their problems together, than with what comparisons could be made with other groups who did not engage in this process.

This pamphlet not only proposes to relate how a number of below-par readers in the junior high school made remarkable strides in reading, but it proposes to tell something about their teachers, too—young people, just out of college—what they learned to do well, what they found successful, and what they found "simply didn't work." The attempt here is to make the story concrete and specific, with the necessary details, so that other teachers can gain insights into problems and procedures which may help them as they tackle a new job with students who seem able to achieve at higher levels, and can rethink and revamp what they already know how to do. The aim is to help teachers gain greater achievement for the children and more satisfaction for themselves. It is designed as an aid to new as well as experienced junior high school teachers when they find themselves confronted with the problem of children who cannot handle the reading materials usually considered suitable for young adolescents. It is an attempt to provide an answer to those who believe that *all* children should learn, and to enable teachers to get started, to organize their classrooms, to learn about children, to learn about materials.

There will probably always be children who leave the elementary school unable to master the reading materials of the junior and senior high schools. At one time, these children would never have been encountered in the secondary schools; they simply dropped out somewhere along the line before that point. Now they are with us and, most certainly within the near future, will continue to be.

Yet, teachers preparing for work in the secondary schools are rarely helped to understand the nature of the reading process, the many and varied causes for individual differences in reading abilities, the increasing differences as children mature, the ways of handling these differences, the destructive effects upon the children of years of failure in learning to read before they reach the junior high school grades, and the many things teachers can do to help children gain some of the ground they have thus far been losing.

Even though the events set forth in these pages took place in a particular school and community, and under a particular set of circumstances, the problems of children and teachers are similar the world over. Everywhere teachers need help if they are to help children. The following pages present a real success story, but the work of the teachers was successful only because they followed certain principles and evolved certain procedures in accordance with those principles.

2 • Classroom Procedures

THE CLASSROOM FACTORS WHICH CONFRONTED THE TEACHERS IN THIS situation were complex. Even though the groups had been "homogeneously" separated from other children with respect to reading achievement, the reading range within each group was tremendous. Some children had no functional word recognition skills. They could recognize isolated words but to put them together in a meaningful context was impossible for them. Others did well in a close-to-fifth-grade reader. The range was also wide with respect to other skills and abilities such as writing, speaking, and using mathematical skills.

Another area showing a wide range was interests, especially those related to reading. Many of the girls wanted "love" stories and career stories; and the boys wanted stories of sports, war, and cowboys. But by no means did all children fall into these categories. Some wanted to read about distant places, others had no idea that books could hold anything of interest to them, while still others continued to be intrigued with animal stories usually written for younger children.

There were wide differences between these children—physical and behavioral, for example. Some children were tall, others tiny; some well developed with respect to secondary sex characteristics; others looked more like children than adolescents, and these were not necessarily the younger ones in the group. Some children were naturally placid and quiet, showing no emotions about anything, or so it seemed; others were high strung and tense, aggressive, and even antisocial. On the surface it might seem that these differences were irrelevant to the reading problem. They were not. In fact, they were closely related to crucial questions teachers ask, such as: "What kind of a book will this child find acceptable?" or "How can the classroom situation be so arranged that all children can learn?"

Then there were vast differences in experiential background. Some children came from families whose vocabulary and speech patterns were

4

such that the children heard a relatively large vocabulary. *Stifle* and *startle* and *emerge* were part of such children's hearing vocabulary. When these youngsters met the word in reading and heard it pronounced, it represented a familiar concept. Some parents took time to explain new things to children; some families visited different places for the sake of their children as well as for their own education and enjoyment. Other children came from families where there was little talk, certainly a minimum of explanation of the ordinary things from which children learn. These children had seldom known what it was like to have their parents read to them. There were few books in their homes, never any discussion of books, rarely the experience of watching a parent enjoy a good book. These things are closely related to children's ability and desire to learn to read, and knowledge of the tremendous range in this particular sphere is of great importance to the teacher who must help the children learn to read.

There was also the whole range of educational experiences through which the child had learned reading. Some had had phonics and more phonics; some had been taught by the word method; others had no recollection at all of how they had been taught to read.

The procedures which were finally evolved had to help solve the problems the teachers faced. The problem of individual differences inherent in the wide range resulting from this multitude of factors in turn posed the problem of an approach which would individualize instruction and not disperse the efforts of the teacher.

PRINCIPLES GUIDING THE PROCEDURES

A framework in which individualization of instruction can go on is of paramount importance

The entire program of an individualized approach was based on the use of a common content theme on which the whole class could focus at any one given period of time. For a number of reasons this was a crucial procedure.

Security for the Teacher

First of all, the common content theme gave to the new teacher, or to the teacher unaccustomed to grappling with the complex problems presented by these children, a firm base from which he could discover and learn to manage an individualized approach to the teaching of reading. This was psychologically sound because these young teachers had themselves been "brought up" on the common text routine with a book report required each month for outside reading. To have every child read a different book, weekly or biweekly, would have been too radical a change. But when children were reading on a common theme of high interest to them, the teacher could help them discuss concepts within the framework of that theme, and could also help them contribute to class understandings from their individual reading experiences. It provided a structured framework of such a nature that, with safety, the teacher could permit and even encourage children to read books of their own choosing. And yet the teacher could handle the situation in a way not too different, at least in outline, from what might be done at certain times in the discussion of any topic. Teachers do discuss various topics with children, whether or not children have read books on them. Sometimes they do it when the children have all read just one book. Now the same kind of discussion was held, but with many books from which to draw information.

For example, let us say that one common theme centers around the topic "What We Learn from Our Families." This is the kind of subject that any teacher might consider with children for any number of reasons, or in any number of contexts. It is a topic which could be discussed whether or not children had read books on it. The children have had, usually, some experiences in family life, as has the teacher. This much is familiar territory for both. Now the teacher can permit the children—encourage them—to bring to the fore new ideas and new perspectives about what we learn from families, perspectives obtained from books. This, of course, follows after discussing with them specifically which books will be of interest to which children. All family stories relate events and incidents through which families educate, even though children have never before considered such incidents in this light, and even though the ways in which they educate are varied.

Opportunities for Every Child to Contribute

The second reason that a common theme was a basic procedure pertains to the fact that it permitted each child to read a book of his own selection. Thus, each child, no matter how poor a reader, could contribute something because he alone, or with two or three others, had read a particular book. He could bring it to the class, knowing that no one else had his special bit of knowledge to contribute. This was quite different from the more usual practice of having discussions solely around a story or a social studies chapter that all children have read, a procedure which can become quite deadening and pointless. In such cases, the child for whom the passage is not too difficult can give the answers to all the questions. If he needs approval of some kind he pays attention and gives those answers; if he does not, he becomes bored and inattentive. Everybody knows the answers because everybody has read the story. Why should he bother? Or, if the story is too difficult, the child meets with frustration in not being able to make a contribution, and if the story is too difficult every day, he meets with constant frustration in reading and in making contributions to the class.

These particular problems are eliminated when teachers plan so that a good portion of the reading is around a common theme. In the situation presented here, the children had read books of interest to them, and on their level, and thus had contributed to the general understandings through their individual reading. And no child felt that his contribution would bore others. What he had to say was unique to the discussion, and he could therefore feel sure that others would want to hear it.

This does not mean that there was no reading and discussion of common stories. There was! But even these were carried on in conjunction with the books of their own choosing which the children were reading. Common readings presented problems of another character, and will be discussed later in this chapter.

Provision for Wide Reading Range and Interest Range

The third argument in favor of the common theme procedure is that if the topic is broad enough—and it is most important that it should be— it can take in a wide reading range and a wide range of subinterests. One class chose "careers" as a topic with the theme or focusing idea being, "The jobs people hold play an important part in all aspects of their lives." For this topic a wealth of career stories was available in many areas, so that all children's interests could be incorporated whether they wanted to be nurses, policemen, auto mechanics, or football coaches. Also, most career stories deal with problems in the areas of living beyond the job itself—the kind of recreation available to a person, or the people the main character meets, or the amount of sleep he can manage to get, or how often he sees his children. Last, but not least, career books are available on a very wide ability level. The *Childhood of Famous Americans Series* has a number of good ones on a fourth-grade reading level; the Sue Barton books, on a sixth.

The class who chose "growing up" and what it means, and where it's "nice" or how it "hurts," also found tremendous possibilities for nurturing individual subinterests and abilities. Children who were interested primarily in independence from parents could find a wealth of characters engaged in solving this problem. Some youngsters seemed to care for little other than "love" stories; still others were already embarked on a common teen-age "I-want-to-reform-the-world" movement. All these subinterests and a multitude more are a part of growing up, and the literature is plentiful. *A Tree for Peter,* by Kate Seredy, is on a fourth-grade level and describes a poverty-stricken youngster of the slums who dreams of becoming an architect who will build beautiful edifices which even the poor will enjoy. *The Red Car,* by Don Stanford, on a sixth-grade level, has an element of striving for independence, yet maintains a feeling of good family relationships.

Opportunity to Develop Basic Ideas

A fourth advantage in using common focusing ideas around which to read is that children can begin to grapple with *ideas* in reading, rather than continue what they have been doing—merely "reading" words. When a class stays with a central theme for a sufficiently long time, teacher and children develop basic notions which become familiar. Children learn to recognize those concepts and to look for variations on them as they read. Reading then becomes meaningful. Children have an opportunity to bring their experiences *to* the reading, and to take new ones *from* the reading, and thus to build up rich concepts of importance to further experiences, whether in reading or in daily living. Such a procedure gives assurance, too, that they will meet the same vocabulary for a space of time long enough to become familiar with it. They are not switching content every day, although each day there is something new in the context. They have ample opportunity to build useful rich ideas and necessary vocabulary. They can become involved in ideas rather than in the struggle for word recognition alone; and the involvement in ideas helps word recognition.

Topics such as "growing up" and "careers" may sound at first like hum-drum, stereotyped subjects, but they are really areas of human interest, and as they are developed conceptually they prove to be rich areas for thought and for reading, for writing and for discussion.

Let us sample some concepts in the topic "Sports and Recreation." What constitutes recreation? It is loafing, doing nothing? How do you know when people are having recreation? Is the same activity recreation for everybody? Why or why not? What happens to people when they recreate? In one child's book, recreation means a chance to "shine" on the ball field; in another, it means an opportunity to use the body freely; in a third, it is the "good feeling" that comes from doing something for somebody; in a fourth, it is the hard labor of building from scratch the racing auto that will be entered in competitions. It is many things, and this is the important point, organizationally, for the classroom teacher. Unless it is many things, there is not sufficient opportunity to play around with a range of ideas over a substantial period of time. Unless it is many things, there is not enough opportunity to cover a breadth of interests. There is room here for the boy who loves sports to read about the thing which is of interest to him, and also for the child who loves music or acting, or for the girl who needs romantic moods.

Freedom to Choose Books

When work is centered around a common theme, the teacher does not have to worry about "checking up on the reading" or about written or oral book reports. He has a record of the books currently being read, and as the group discussion proceeds, he can stimulate and encourage the children to make their contributions.

Excerpts from a taped discussion will serve to demonstrate this procedure. The concept being examined was that families protect children in a variety of ways in order to help them grow up with a feeling of security. The teacher had read aloud "The Shanahan Strad" by Paul Jones[1] and had discussed with the children their reactions to this kind of protection. Together they had examined ways in which they knew real families do this, and what they liked or disliked about the way these families did these things. Of course, the group opinion was split and so the concept needed to be examined further for conditions under which this kind of "protection" was advisable. The children had been given a list of family stories from which to select books for independent reading and now the time for further consideration of the problem was upon them: Should families protect children from knowing certain facts about the family situation?

PAUL: In *Mama's Bank Account* she tells the kids a lie about a bank account. There isn't even a bank account but she keeps telling the kids there is; I just hated her. I despise her.

[1] In Eric Berger, *Best Short Shorts* (Englewood Cliffs, N. J.: *Readers' Choice*, Scholastic Book Services, a division of Scholastic Magazines, Inc., 1958).

ADOLPH: I don't see why you should despise her. She was trying to get the children to feel safe. She wanted them to feel safe. So she made up a bank account. Then the children wouldn't worry.

PAUL: I despise her. It's a downright lie. I'd hate my mother to tell me a lie like that. She thought she was so big and everything.

TEACHER: Do you think perhaps the age of the child makes a difference in the kind of protection he needs?

*   *   *

DOREEN: My book is *Caddie Woodlawn.* The father was protecting the girl. In a way he was. After the mother punished her he sat down with her and talked with her. He didn't turn on the light and he didn't make her open her eyes or say 'Look at me; I'm talking to you.' Nothing like that. He knew she was feeling bad.

KATHY: He made her feel better because now she had someone on her side.

DOREEN: He wasn't on her side, but he wasn't against her.

TEACHER: Do you mean that in the way he talked to her she knew she wasn't completely alone, that someone did care about her even though she had to be punished, and that this is a kind of protection?

The teacher may fear that such procedures mean he must read all the books the children are reading. This is quite impossible, because he cannot keep up with thirty different children reading, as is the aim, a book every week or two. More than that, to attempt to do so is fatal because then the children must be prevented from reading books the teacher has not read. It would mean that the children cannot have freedom to read what is of interest to them; it is a frustrating and stultifying procedure. Instead of adopting such a restraining measure, the teacher can use a more positive approach, such as involving children in an activity in which they are really needed. Compiling an annotated bibliography for next year's class is an activity of this type. One way to get this started is to submit to the children a fairly limited list. The children's bibliography may not only be annotated but books may be rated as far as degree of interest is concerned.

Guide for Daily Lesson Planning

Planning for reading on individual levels around a common theme has an additional advantage which gives security to the teacher. Although considerable preliminary planning is required, the daily lessons fall into line. It is readily apparent as a result of one day's lesson just what is required for the next. This is a boon for the young teacher, who all too often becomes bogged down in worries about "What shall I do tomorrow?" The theme has already been decided upon for a relatively long span of lessons. The problem is, specifically, what focusing ideas are to be built around it, what skills must be planned, and how will those ideas be used to further skills training? For example, let us take the previously mentioned theme of "careers." On the first day one teacher talked with the children about what their parents did for a living, how they liked what they did, what the children thought they themselves would choose for careers, how they knew this was what they wanted. Then, for an assignment, they were asked to interview an adult on what his job consisted of, how he happened to have chosen it, what preparation he had had for it, what he liked or disliked about it. From the data the children brought back, several concepts were evolved with the help of the teacher. "Jobs make a difference in all parts of people's lives" (this was evolved from the question on likes and dislikes), "There are many reasons why people stay with a job even though they dislike it," "Some people seem to have had more opportunities than others in preparing for and finding a satisfying job."

The children wrote up their interviews with the help of the teacher because the data would be needed later for reference when children checked and rechecked and considered more carefully the same concepts. The concepts were seen more or less as hypotheses at this stage and much more evidence needed to be gathered from books. Then the teacher handed out a list of about forty annotated books on careers. Some were love stories, others adventure stories; some very simple, others a bit more difficult—but all emphasized careers. That was the reading lesson for the day, to read the annotated list and try to decide which book would appeal to whom. The teacher had library copies of many of these books. In one case the teacher and the neighborhood librarian had worked together, compiling the list, and the introduction of the books in conjunction with reading the list was done by the librarian. In another instance, the teacher read parts of the books and talked about them with the children. The teacher's chief problem at this point was to steer away from the difficult books those children who could not handle them and help them become interested in easier ones. Reading exciting parts of the easier books and talking about "trying a book on for fit"[2] were effective means of influencing some children. The children were asked to decide, by reading at home, whether or not the chosen books were interesting enough for them to want to continue.

[2] This procedure is described in greater detail later in this chapter.

The children came in the next day with their books (the teacher was prepared for "forgetters" and had a few extra books on hand). Of the children who did not like the books they had selected, some insisted on continuing with them while others asked the teacher to exchange their books. Those who had read enough to know that a book was of interest read silently or to their "partners." The teacher went from one to the other, listening to them read, helping them to overcome hurdles, sharing their stories with them, recording errors and needs for near-future lessons.

The teacher then read aloud a short story which did the content job needed at this point. The interviews with adults which the children had held earlier had brought out certain basic concepts. But these concepts had to be reconsidered because in a sense they were being held as hypotheses. Children had found, for example, that most people gave strong reactions to elements of their jobs which they disliked, yet they stayed with them. Some people did not seem to feel "proud of themselves." Then why did they not leave one job and go to another? The story the teacher read aloud was chosen for the purpose of helping the children see that there were new facts not brought out by interviews but nevertheless pertinent to the major concept. "The Ordeal," by Norman Katkov,[3] told of a twelve-year-old boy who was ashamed of the work his father did and the story showed other ways in which the father's job influenced the family. New perspectives were here. Children discussed how they felt about parents' jobs, or talked about "people they knew" who felt certain ways about their parents' jobs. The teacher turned the discussion to the effect of all of this on the breadwinner and on his motives and feelings. She then explained to the children that they might look for this idea in their books. One child had read enough of his book the previous night to "think his book would be about that."

From this point on there were other stories which the children could read themselves, common stories to be done with the help of the teacher, stories which would clarify and enrich the other concepts already somewhat explored. Thus, the concepts helped the children bring understanding to the books they were reading, so that their books could in turn add something new to their understandings. And since concepts were usually held as hypotheses, to be examined for validity through life and literature, the children needed the additional experiences with which to examine them.

The reader can see how these steps were evolved logically, naturally, from what went before. Because the teacher had done thorough long-

---

[3] Reprinted in *Literature For Life* by Arno Jewett, A. H. Lass, and Margaret Early (Boston: Houghton Mifflin Co., 1958), pp. 329–339.

term preplanning, because the concepts were the guide around which all was built, the daily activities, the short-term planning, "came naturally." The teacher began by encouraging children to talk about what they "wanted to be" and how they knew this. Many did not know. Then how do people decide? This question led logically to finding out from adults who were already engaged in careers. The planned interview became the "natural" next step. Children brought back information which had to be examined systematically. This led to formulation of certain generalizations or concepts. But there were contradictory pieces of evidence and there were gaps in knowledge. So the concepts were really hypotheses. Then how could children make sure? Look further! Books could help. So short stories read in common with the teacher showed how books really did help, and individual reading on the child's own level of interest and ability came into play. Each activity virtually dictated what the next should be.

The concepts which are chosen as a focus for instruction must be comprehensive as well as important to children and to society

Once the teachers understood the organization of the work they had few difficulties in carrying it out. The chief problem was gaining an understanding of what a concept is, of the importance of stating it clearly to themselves as a guide for future planning, of the urgency of arriving at concepts of interest and importance to children and to the society at large, and of the necessity for working with themes which were comprehensive. The tendency at first was to frame "should" concepts. For example, on the subject of careers teachers tended to think in these terms: "We should prepare carefully for the job we want." This kind of thinking is disastrous to the program for a number of reasons: (1) Though literature does teach, it is not a means of moralizing. If the teacher wishes to moralize, that is a separate problem, and should be removed from literature. (2) We want children to enjoy books, to go to them for what they want to know. Children rarely go to books to be "preached to." (3) In addition, a "should" concept forces the distortion of the meaning of the author to make it conform to what the teacher has in mind.

Primarily, what is sought is a concept which is a true generalization and which permits creative thinking on the child's part about what he can bring to the book and what he carries away from it. Such a concept might be "Jobs affect people's lives in many ways," "There are personal and community forces which help and/or hinder in the attainment of careers individuals seek." These are the adult terms in which the teacher states them as he plans, but later he helps children frame concepts in their own terms after they have engaged in experiences which permit them to do so, experiences such as the interviews with adults cited earlier. Concepts like "Jobs affect people's lives in many ways" require no distortion of the author's purpose. Either the author does tell about one of these concepts or about the other, or he tells about neither.

In a sense, teachers of reading must be curriculum builders, at least to a limited degree. The procedures described in this pamphlet demonstrate this. The reading teachers must absorb basic ideas in literature and life, a true curriculum building process which their sociology background should encourage. Teachers take some of these basic ideas with which they are already deeply imbued and use them as a central focus or a framework around which to help each individual child find his way into reading on his own level, to his own taste, according to his own interests. This means, of course, that these originally determined ideas in literature must first be tested for pertinence to children and for pertinence to available books on cross-difficulty levels. It is only as the teacher comes to know what is pertinent in the lives of children and what materials and resources are available through which these things can be taught, that he can program individualized reading, individualized approaches.

Once the teacher learns how to state a concept clearly and how to build several related concepts, he has direction for his search of specific books. Once he has tapped the interests of individual children and the levels at which they can read without too much assistance, he is already providing for his charges an individualized approach with solid foundations through which each child can learn to read—and like it—and through which the teacher can move with a very real measure of security to himself and to the children. The process of focusing on an important concept permits children to function as a class group, does not separate one from the other in all areas and categories of their reading task. Even though some are reading on a second-grade level while others are on a fifth, they are reading about essentially the same basic ideas, which permits them to communicate easily.

Instructional processes to be used must be evaluated for their ability to foster wide reading by the children

Teachers in the school situation described here discovered that their underachievers in reading had previously been taught phonics, had been given drills and exercises, but had not read widely on their own levels and to their own tastes. Rarely, if ever, did a child report that he had read a book on his own, no matter how few pages it contained. Rarely did he report experiences with classrooms that had their own small libraries which even he was encouraged and given time to use. The teachers felt, therefore, that much and varied practice through the reading of many books on an individual difficulty level and high interest level and with real motivation to read would bring appreciable improvement in reading skills over a period of two years. They used formalized practice exercises only where absolutely necessary, only where they served a vital purpose. They believed in highly motivated and varied practice, but in minimal drill. Another reason for this principle was that they hoped to help even these slow readers gain the reading habit, the enjoyment of books at whatever level. They aimed for this despite the fact that the attitudes of the children toward anything looking like a book were negative. The teachers were not antipractice. They believed in it wholeheartedly if it made sense to the child and met his needs. They *were* antidrill of a formalized disconnected nonsense-to-the-child nature. They were opposed to merely repetitive drill and believed children would drill themselves if they set the stage for it through motivated practice, through reading and still more reading. This meant something more than exercise books with one paragraph and ten questions about it on a page. With such a routine, children could never "get off the ground." They were always reading in the slow, emotionally uninvolved way one reads the first paragraph of a new novel in contrast to the sweeping pace with which the eye consumes page after page once the reader is absorbed. The teachers wanted the children to have a chance to become absorbed.

Reading instruction must be so planned as to give every child an equal opportunity to learn

Boards of education usually provide teachers with course of study guides. These in a very real sense are important aids to teachers, especially as a security-giving device. Sometimes, however, teachers follow them so closely as to permit little or no flexibility for meeting the needs of the children for whose welfare the guides were originally intended. Teachers need to learn how to use these guides in a sensible manner so that the security element is still there for them, while the possibilities for flexibility must be put to use if the guides are to serve the children's needs, too. Also, teachers must learn how to use the guide in such a way that reading instruction is achieved within the context of some of the content described in it. This is so, no matter what subject area it may be—English, social studies, core program, science, or what-have-you. But, more important, it must be remembered that equal opportunity for education does not mean all children must learn the same things at the same time. When teachers attempt to interpret guides as aids in helping children learn the same things at the same time, thinking that this means children are receiving an equal opportunity for education, they are disappointed in the results. Actually, those procedures will bring about unequal opportunities. Since the interests and abilities a child develops are different from those of other children, what he can learn at a given time is not the same as what others can learn either in content or in amount. A child forced to read content too difficult for him, or at a rate too fast for him, is being denied equal opportunity to learn. One required to spend time waiting for others to get to the point which he reached long ago also is being denied equal opportunity to learn. If a course of study is interpreted so rigidly that every child must learn the same thing at the same time and in the same amounts, this is a travesty on equal opportunity for education because it denies him the right to learn what he *can* learn at a given time. So, teachers must acquire know-how in using courses of study creatively. Most courses do allow for creativity, but teachers, in their uncertainty about themselves and the classroom situation, use them as an excuse for not being flexible, for not recognizing individual needs and meeting them. The excuse is used in all sincerity. But until teachers learn that it is possible to be creative under the circumstances, and until they learn how to do this, the cry will continue to be heard, "But we can't do this or that because we have to cover content." An age-old cry. Using a course of study creatively is not an easy problem in view of the fact that children want to feel they are studying the same basic things as are their classmates. This desire, in fact, is another reason for keeping to the prescribed course of study in basic outline. The children want to be treated as the others are; they are not different from them in most respects. They are aware of what goes on in other classes; they feel cheated if they do not "have" the same things. Often, their aspirations are not far removed from some of the others. Knowing that others are studying "Our Community" will cause them to doubt themselves much more than they already do if they are not permitted also to engage in this same study.

The use of common content ideas as a central focus for planning experiences needed by the children is one very important way to use the study guides flexibly.

Every procedure selected for use must be evaluated for its fruitfulness in fostering good mental health

There was constant concern with the mental health of the children and its relationship to their sense of achievement in reading. It was necessary that the teachers learn to do only those things which fostered good mental health of children. It was not known whether the difficulties children encountered in reading were based—at least in part—on emotional problems; nor was it known whether the present emotional problems of so many of them came, rather, from early and continued all-over patterns of failure connected with reading. It *was* apparent that both factors— emotional difficulties and reading problems—were often if not usually present. It was believed that if children could gain a sense of achievement in reading, their mental health would show a degree of improvement, manifested in a number of ways—in their gaining new interests about which they could become excited instead of continuing to give lethargic responses; in their "sudden" awakening to the fact that they could now uncover something that had always been a frustrating mystery; in their new desire to want to push ahead their own learning as evidenced in requests to take books home; in their greater pride in doing well whatever jobs they did undertake; in their expression of goals; in their decreasing antisocial behavior; in their increasing social behavior; in their spontaneous asking of questions in place of the attitude "I couldn't care less"— all these and more.

Such things as the usual paper-and-pencil tests served little purpose. The kind that was useful was the open-ended type which permitted children to respond as they would. Parents' reactions were also important, especially concerning how they felt about what their children were now able to do. Through procedures such as these, and through careful observation, the teachers noted growth in the children's mental health.

Teachers came to recognize that the learning power they hoped to achieve in the children required a concept of teaching which involved much more than merely "telling" them. It would not be accomplished if they thought of teaching as merely holding children captive in order to "pour in" information. It was necessary for children to go out, to reach out, to find out what they needed to know. This did not mean that teachers could never "tell" or that children never learned by having the teacher tell. It did mean that if learning was to be active, telling could not be the prime method. When children needed to know something and were aware of this fact, the teacher's telling was a response to their need, and the process could thus be active learning. If a child knew that his weakness in reading was in figuring out the meaning of the new word from the context, and if, whenever he read, he set about using the skills introduced by his teacher to help him over this hurdle, he was engaged in active learning. Children *knowing* what they needed to know, children knowing how to get the information or acquire the skill, and children going about the business of their own learning were elements emphasized in the program.

The concern for mental health also forced a reconsideration of children's second-year assignment to teachers. It was hoped that teachers with one year of in-service help would go on with the children to the next grade so that these children would have the benefit of what the teacher now knew and was able to do, which she previously had not been able to do. Also, teachers would know the children and time would be saved because they could pick up in September where they had left off. The children needed this extra measure of security. Knowing that there would be one out of their several teachers who knew them and who cared about them would add strength to the psychological growth it was hoped would take place. It must never be forgotten that the children had been stamped as failures for years. It had taken weeks and even months to convince some of them that they could learn to read. It was thought that the school ought not take a chance on the possibility of regression with respect to this factor. It was assumed, too, that because of the details discussed above it would take at least two years for children to show an appreciable achievement. In these two years the teacher, too, would have time to grow with the children.

ACHIEVING EARLY SUCCESS

Teachers had very specific goals which helped them meet their major objectives of teaching children to read, to enjoy reading, and to gain the reading habit. One of these goals was to bring about early success, to give the feeling that now in a new school there was a new beginning.

A Project with Juvenile Books

One way of ensuring early success was through the use of younger children's books. Many of these junior high school children could not read books of interest to them because in certain areas there are not suffi-cient numbers available with easy vocabularies. Therefore, it was necessary for the teacher to make easy books acceptable to these children, books of a more childish nature which they would ordinarily find insulting to their intelligence, to themselves as human beings growing into adulthood. Projects were organized around the use of little children's books. One class read such books to study the degree to which the author used the element of horror. Was there too much horror for little children? Was a book too "soupy" and lacking in "spice?" The teacher read them some psychologically oriented newspaper articles on the effect of fear on little children, and even some paragraphs from a psychology textbook. The children felt "grown-up" at thus being taken into the confidence of adults as equals. They read book after book. When at least six children had read a book, they gathered together to discuss and "officially" rate that book for the edification of parents. A one-sentence annotation was composed, a horror rating given, and the book was classified as recommended or not recommended. A bibliography for parents was prepared, mimeographed, and distributed to parents of younger children.

There were variations of this activity. One class studied "fantasy" in little children's books and tried to decide whether it was "a good kind"; another group became intrigued with endings of stories and tried to decide whether or not the endings they liked now as compared with those little children liked gave any indications that they had grown up.

The children were told why it was important for them to read "easier-than-they-wanted-to" books. In simple terms, the teacher explained how the eye works during the reading process, showed what happens to its performance when the reader meets too difficult or too many unfamiliar words. The children were aiming now at fluency, and fluency is gained when the eye is permitted freedom to move easily. The children loved these short technical explanations; they "made sense."

Since the books to be included in the bibliography had to be rated, and since the children who had read a particular book often could not agree on the evaluation, it was usually necessary for them to read their selections to younger children. To prepare for reading to younger siblings or neighborhood children, there was much preliminary reading and re-reading and "practicing on each other." The book had to be read well in order to get a true reaction. The class discussed what kinds of reactions they would look for. At what point does the child ask a question? Where is his excitement greatest? Where does his interest lag? Does he seem amused, or is he really frightened? How do you know?

Here is an excerpt from a discussion with one of the teachers: "The children began the session without waiting for me to start the ball rolling. They couldn't wait to report on their success with reading to their younger siblings or neighbors. I used this opportunity to ask them to write about this experience. Later, as they talked, one child repeated that her brother had asked for it again and again, until she had to distract him to another activity. Another child read a book in which appeared the words 'strut' and 'waddle'. When I asked her how she managed to explain such hard words she said, 'I showed him'. And I complimented her on her ability as a teacher. I'm finding the use of easy books for reading to younger children an outstanding stimulus. Some of the children are even beginning to be amazingly relaxed with reading."

Though the children accepted the project wholeheartedly, much of this reading had to be done in school time, because many of the children, boys especially, would not "be caught dead" carrying a "baby book." Others had no fear about being seen with such an object. For the boys who "cared" we quickly found such books as *Squanto and the Pilgrims* (Harper & Rowe), and the Bobbs-Merrill *Childhood of Famous Americans Series*. These are more adult in content but at third- and fourth-grade reading levels.

Whether the class as a whole accepts and enjoys the sibling-book project depends to a large extent on the way the teacher handles it. That they do enjoy it is obvious from the following excerpts from a taped recording:[4]

MIKE: I compared the book to [with] two different little kids. I read it to one and then to another one, and I read one in the morning and one in the night, and I think it was good because they liked it because the one in the night didn't yawn. They were like this: "What's gonna happen next?" You know, they were lookin' like that.

*   *   *

MARILYN: The title of mine is *Play With Me*. When I first opened it, I made sure it has big letters so if they look on with me they can almost read it themselves. And they have big pictures in here.

*   *   *

CAROLINE: I read to a neighbor's little boy and little girl. The little boy was four, so I said to him . . . "Did you like the story" and he said, "Yeah because he won the prize," and all that.

TEACHER: What was the title of the book you read?

CAROLINE: *Bugs Bunny at the Country Fair*. The seven-year-old started reading it to me at first, and I told her that I gotta read it to her. She can read very good.

*   *   *

[4] From a recording of a discussion led by Mr. Eli Seifman.

MIKE: Sunday I didn't have anything to do so I took out the book and I read it to my brothers, my two brothers and next-door neighbor's two children. It's by Dr. Seuss, *One Fish, Two Fish, Red Fish, Blue Fish.* Well, my brothers liked it because it rhymed and because there's two characters in it, Joe and Mike, that—y'know my brother's name is Joe, so they laughed and said it was *us.* They just enjoyed it, but the other boy and girl are in school—one is five and one in first grade. So the older one stood there reading it, and when I came to a part that this girl liked she almost memorized it.

Then I read another book, *The Cat in the Hat.* This was a story like, but it rhymed and they liked this more than *One Fish, Two Fish.*

TEACHER: How do you explain the fact that they liked one better if they are both by the same author?

MIKE: This book is just riddles and it doesn't have a very good ending, y'know, to the story. But in the other story the cat comes back and he cleans the house up and then they see the mother, and the mother asks how they kept the house so clean.

THOMAS: I'm surprised at that because usually when you go into a regular bookstore for children they always recommend Dr. Seuss books for children because they are so interesting and hold their interest.

TEACHER: That's right. Mike did say that the children liked both but they liked *Cat in the Hat* even better. Was that right, Mike?

MIKE: Yes, and George has *Cat in the Hat Comes Back;* it's the same thing, but continuous.

TEACHER: Maybe we can hear from George now. Did you read it to your young child yet, George?

GEORGE: I brought the child five books and let him pick, and he picked out *Cat in the Hat* and I read it to him. He started to read some too, and made a few mistakes. He liked the little cats; he had a whole bunch of baby cats under his hat and he liked that. It's like a trick, keeping a whole bunch of cats under the hat like that. . . .

TEACHER: Did he understand the ending?

GEORGE: Yes, he did, because he was the one that read it to me. I let him read that part. . . . He said "I like that last cat."

HILDA: I had the book, *Daddy's Picnic and other Stories* and just read *Daddy's Picnic* to my next-door neighbor. She liked it because she said they had a good time. And she understood the ending because she laughed and clapped her hands.

TEACHER: Did anyone have any unusual experiences when you tried to read your book?

ROBERT: Yeah. You know, I have that book *Yogi Bear* that Brenda gave me, so my cousin came over and she's a pretty smart kid, so my sister let the bird out of the house and the kid followed the bird and paid no attention to the story.

*   *   *

SANDY: (About the book *Dumbo*) When I got to the middle of the book she ran away and started to fly around like the elephant, and I couldn't stop her.

TEACHER: What does that tell us about one of the answers we are looking for?

MARTY: She understood the story, because she goes flying around chairs and making believe her ears were wings.

* * *

TEACHER: Did anyone else have an unusual experience?

MARTY: I had a bird book, like Sandy's only a little bigger but not many words in it. I read about all the birds in the winter go South and he starts crying, because he's so sorry they went South. He's really mixed up, and then I read on and it says in the end Spring will be here and all the birds will be back, and he yells "hurrah hurrah."

ANTHONY: I was reading the story to my brother and stopped in the middle to ask him questions and he said, "Shut up, Andy, and finish reading the story." He wouldn't let me ask any more questions.

* * *

TEACHER: What sorts of endings seem to be the type that the children like?

CORINNE: I found they like happy endings like the ending of *Bugs Bunny* when he won the biggest prize and all that. They like happy endings, not when someone dies, and mysteries.

BONNIE: When the story is finished and they say the princess lives happily ever after. They want to know what happened—is she going to have children after that. They want the story to continue.

There are evidences here not only of the children's enjoyment, but of what they are learning about human behavior as well as about reading. For some, this was a new and real effort on their part to make a relationship with other human beings. It was new in the sense that to make warm relationships was difficult for them. Now they were receiving fresh satisfactions in this area of their lives. There is evidence, too, of their seriousness about the project. The readers can see the aims of the teacher. From this point on he could lead them to see the need for other classmates to read the same books to other small children and to discuss how they themselves felt about the endings of those books. He could read short stories to the whole class. He could use the books the children were discussing to consider basic ideas such as: Should books for little children be "true to life"? Did teen-agers want everything to end happily? Was it "true to life" for family members never to quarrel? What *was* the meaning of "true to life"? Or he could lead them into a consideration of certain specific aspects of human behavior, using their observations of the little children to do this.

Selecting the Appropriate Book

Achieving the goal of early success at this crucial time in a new school required other things of the teachers, too. When children were reading on their own levels and, where feasible and desirable, were reading a common story, teachers learned to read *to* children until they became emotionally involved in their story, and then let them proceed on their own wherever possible. In doing this, they hoped that the momentum would carry them along. Their hopes were usually satisfied if the story was properly selected. Teachers also learned to do the reverse of what their inclination might be: to permit and even encourage children to read books that could be finished at a few not-too-long sittings rather than to expect them to read a book with many pages. "Skinny" books became acceptable.

Teachers realized that a book must never be permitted to drag on for a long time. They read with the child (or found a "partner" to read with him) to help him finish it in a reasonably short time; or they took it away and started him on, plunged him into, an easier, shorter one. This function seems a simple one to learn. Actually, it was one of the most difficult things for all teachers. In the first place, their acquaintance with children's books was so meager that they had no framework within which to make judgments quickly, almost on the spot, about what constituted a third-grade level book, or a fourth, or a fifth. Children came in with pocketbooks their big brothers were reading and tenaciously held on to them, refusing to surrender them for easier ones (except within the previously described project using younger children's books). At first there was almost complete unawareness on the part of a teacher that this book was quite impossible for that child. When he did realize it, such devices as the one cited above in which the teacher talked about eye-span helped some. Then, the teacher explained to children how to try a book on for "fit." If they missed more than two words in a large paragraph, and felt that they were not "getting" the story, this was not a good "fit." This rule of thumb helped in a limited number of cases. It was necessary to give daily demonstrations of books that were suitable. When teachers were sure that a particular book and child suited each other, the child read for the class and the performance was discussed.

Using the "Experience" Story

Working with a common theme helped meet the goal of early success in another way, too, this time with the nonreader. There were three or four children in each group who could not read at all, or at least claimed they could not, and test results bore out their statements, sometimes because they simply marked the test "any old way," knowing they would not do well, or in other cases because they did not understand directions or because they really had no word recognition ability. With these children, it was necessary to work especially quickly to demonstrate that reading was a possibility for them also. For these, teachers used an adaptation of the "experience story" used by primary-grade teachers, but here it was on an individual basis. The teacher acted as the child's "secretary" during a period when others were writing and took down, verbatim, his story. This was given a title, the "author" was named, and the story was typed double or triple spaced in duplicate. Next day, the teacher gave one copy to the child and from the other she read to him as he watched his own. Usually there was a broad smile of real pleasure at seeing himself "in print" and listening to his own story being read. Almost invariably, the child was able to read his own story back to the teacher with a minimum of errors if too much time had not elapsed between creating it and reading it. The reason, of course, was that it was his own vocabulary, his own flow of words, and that he knew the content since it was his. Now he had just the mechanics to contend with, and he could handle the situation. Almost invariably there was a terrific boost to morale at this demonstration that he could learn to read. This process was continued under a variety of circumstances. A student teacher took over, or another child, a sociometric choice,[5] acted as his secretary for future stories, and later copied the teacher's technique of marking the words he had missed and of helping him to learn to recognize them. The child-secretary took his story down from dictation when the teacher was too busy with other things involving the whole class. An example of such a story follows.

RIDING TO SCHOOL IN THE RAIN
BY JOHN DOE

When I was coming from my house to school, I was in the rain. The rain was coming down in buckets and buckets. I was on my bike. I was riding to school. It was really coming down, the rain. My mother told me not to go to school because it was raining too hard. But I rode to school on my bike in the rain. The rain was coming down in buckets and buckets.

When I came to the school, I saw my friend. My friend's name is Tommy. Tommy came to school with his mother. Tommy's mother drove Tommy to school.

[5] See Helen Hall Jennings, *Sociometry in Group Relations,* Revised Edition (Washington, D.C.: American Council on Education, 1959).

When I took off my raincoat, I went to the water fountain to get a drink of water because I could not get a drink of water from the rain. Then my teacher and I[6] started to work with my reading. We worked on our words and we read the story I wrote last week. I got plenty of words wrong. I hope I don't get many wrong when I read this story.

Often children do not like to dictate personal stories. When the class is discussing a theme and the concepts around it have been built up in such a way that daily experiences of all children can be brought to it, getting an "experience" story is not difficult. If the class is discussing careers, and the children have held an interview with an adult engaged in the career the child thinks he would like, it is a simple matter to get a story out of him. The teacher need not worry about whether he is a "verbal" child or not, whether he will "give" or not. He now has something to say, and saying is no problem for him. Or if the class is talking and writing about ways in which families educate, and children are discussing younger siblings and observing them, and are observing what families do teach them informally by the way they talk with them and play with them and feed them, stories come readily. This focus has an added advantage: All the children are making a contribution to group ideas, and this child is not left out because he cannot read or write. It is still his story, even though someone else at the moment is doing the mechanical recording of it. If, on occasion, the contributions of all the children are mimeographed, for all to read, every class member feels he is receiving equal attention.

Teachers in the project also found that they need not wait for perfection before praising a child sincerely, but could note each little element of progress and could help the children be aware of this and of what it meant. Teachers had to learn not to let a day go by without making a hopeful and genuinely encouraging remark to the class as well as to individuals. Such a remark could be on paper or directly stated face to face, but it was necessary in some form to the morale of the children. However, mere encouragement and support without tangible achievement results were fruitless. Children had to see and feel that they were learning, were making progress.

INTEGRATION OF THE LANGUAGE ARTS

Many other sound procedures for helping children improve their ability to read were facilitated by the use of the common content theme

[6] Child said "me" but teacher "edited."

as the basic procedure. For example, one important aspect of organizing the work to help children's progress in reading was integration of the language arts. The things talked about in class, the films shown as topics of conversation and written work, were around the same subject as that chosen for reading so that word meanings and whole ideas could be gained and concepts deepened.

Writing

There was much, much writing. Not a day went by without some writing. This meant finding reasons for this activity which were real to the children. Those words which they were seeing in print were now being used by them, a process which fortified their reading skills. But more than that, the ideas gained in reading were being emphasized, and new ideas and concepts which would bring richness to their reading were being developed.

Reasons for writing were both "natural" and contrived. Children wrote, and did not mind correcting even a number of times, "stories" to be mimeographed so the whole class could read them. For example, "The Most Frightening Time of My Life" was the subject of one. This came within the context of the books they were reading in connection with their study of "horror in little children's books." The papers they wrote were corrected and mimeographed—everybody's, unless a child requested that his be kept confidential. There was a maximum of intense interest when the copies of the "booklet" were distributed, and this became the reading lesson for the day. Children talked to each other about what each frightening experience meant, there were many questions asked of each other, and the teacher led the discussion into channels which would enrich their understanding.

Even the children with grade-two reading levels wrote when the motivation was there—and did this without "secretaries." Here is an illustration of a "true story" written by a girl whose reading level was 2.3. As the children wrote, the teacher moved around the room giving whatever assistance was necessary with spelling or other mechanical stumbling blocks the children were encountering.

WHAT I DON'T UNDERSTAND ABOUT GROWNUPS

What can we do to make our mothers and fathers understand about love? When I want to go out, my mother and father says, "Stay in." My mother says, "I'll give you a boy on the head." I say that I love the boy. My father starts to yell. I walk out and when I come in my father tells me to do my homework.

Last night my brother told me to stay in with my father. I brought my friends inside. I said, "This is the boy I love." I'll not mention any names because he goes to this school. He is in class 7-S. His room number is 489.

At other times they talked and wrote of their observations of young children's reactions to the books they read to them. This was done in connection with the children's bibliography project, when the pupils found they needed tangible evidence for the record to help in making the final evaluation of each book. These written pieces of evidence were kept until five or six children had read the book and then these same children formed a committee which used the written evidence in rating the book as being appropriate or inappropriate for little children. All writing activities had a purpose real to the children.

Sometimes teachers used an idea to stimulate creative writing simply because it was an idea which they felt would appeal to the children. They did this even though at first the work was not correlated with the reading and discussions in which children were engaged at the moment. However, the teacher's ingenuity and planning led to a strengthening of the ties between the writing and the reading. For example, one teacher began a method which so intrigued the children that they continued it for a far longer span of time than she had ever intended. One day, she wrote four phrases on the board:

> pack of cigarettes
> discarded can of sardines
> dim street lamp
> kerchief

and proceeded to read a story woven around these phrases, a story which she had created but which the children thought was written by an "author." Then she led a discussion on what the children thought about the story, and was surprised at the depth of understanding about what makes a good story, for they were extremely critical and could generally be led to give reasons for each criticism. When she told them it was *her* creation, there was crestfallen silence and a feeling that this was not quite cricket. But when she explained that she feared they would not have been frank with her otherwise and that she, in turn, would be frank with them when they wrote, everything was "all right" again.

Next she put new phrases on the board:

> a broken pair of scissors
> a torn flag
> a crumpled letter
> a cast-off newspaper
> a shriveled old lady

One child pointed to his broken arm which was in a cast, as if to help her with her list. The children were all eager to write, even the nonwriters. Enough excitement had been generated for that. For the first few minutes they were completely engrossed in their task. Then began the need to share their creations. One boy nudged another and said, "See what I wrote." But the second boy was still busy and could not be bothered. The teacher at this point said, "I'll call time in a few minutes. Meantime don't disturb the others if you are finished. Everyone will have a chance to share his story with others."

The teacher called "time" before all the class had completed their stories and there was a roar of protest. But she promised time to finish later. One or two children read their stories; they were discussed and enjoyed (not evaluated to the extent that hers was), and then the children divided into groups to enjoy those written by others and to have theirs enjoyed. A few were chosen to share with the whole class, chosen by the children in groups according to criteria established with the children beforehand. Such criteria could be the "tallness" of the tall tale, or interesting beginnings, or surprise endings. Criteria had to be limited in number. Every child's composition was read but the whole class did not have to listen to all thirty of them, so there was no waste of time; there was wise use of class time. There was seriousness of purpose. The papers were so good that they were later used for intensive individual correction and mimeographed for a future reading lesson. (There was nothing personal here, so it was safe to use this procedure.)

The children enjoyed this activity so much that the teacher suggested they keep a little slip of paper as a bookmark in the books they were reading and, when they came across an expression or phrase which particularly intrigued them, jot it down to share with the class for writing purposes. Lists became so long that the next time a preliminary committee had to be chosen to limit the items to fifteen from which the children could choose.

A variation was suggested by the children when they read biographies. Two children read one biography. Each partner drew up his own secret list of phrases. On the day set for writing each gave his list to the other as a guide for writing the life of their great man.

Other writing experiences followed, each with emphasis on enjoyment, so children would want to continue to write. Children were assigned the task of finding incidents in their books which posed problems for people. This meant some previous intensive work with them by the teacher before they were able to carry out such an assignment. The teacher read several short stories and several excerpts from novels, before they were able to grasp the idea. When each child had selected his problematic situation from his own book they met in groups to select one. The incidents chosen were presented in a read-and-tell method to the whole class who selected one for which they would like to act out creative solutions.

Several role-playing situations were acted out and discussed. Then, each child chose the one he liked best and wrote on why he felt it presented the best solution to the problem. If he felt none of them was feasible, he could write one that was.

In a book called *Teen-Age Companion*[7] there is a story, "Top of the Mountain." When the teacher read this to the climax, it was one of such appeal to children of this age that they wrote easily about its possible ending, and really enjoyed doing it. Then the teacher read the ending and they discussed it together, after which two or three of the children's endings were read and discussed according to certain limited criteria. One such criterion was logical consequence: Does the ending follow as an outgrowth of what went before? Another teacher used the criterion, Is it true to life?

There were situations, however, where this method of selecting a child's story to be read to the whole class simply did not work. Such occasions occurred when the children were still so insecure that they could not "afford" to choose someone else's, when there were children who had never yet appeared "in print." This happened in the room of one teacher who made a practice of mimeographing only a select few of the children's stories, so that most children were never given an opportunity to be the chosen ones. Neither did this practice work when children were thrown together at random rather than by choice. But in classes where some self-confidence was already built, where the relation with the teacher was warm, children could tolerate this amount of competition. Otherwise, it proved far better to use groups to *help* each other, to put together several heads to assist each writer in meeting the criteria better than he had.

Other writing situations occurred in connection with predictions of what would happen in a story. This differed from the previously described procedure in which the teacher read to the climax and then had children write the ending. Here the teacher read with them up to an interesting point to help them plunge into the story. Then they discussed "whether you think Squanto will get away." Following this they wrote their own opinions and kept them until they read to see how correct were their guesses. If a common story was being read, children could keep a running record of their success in predicting. Later, they did it on their own

[7] Frank Owen, *Teen-Age Companion* (New York: Lantern Press, Inc., 1946).

with their individual books. It worked especially well where two children were reading the same book and sharing their written predictions. This whole procedure was also good motivation for reading more frequently and for longer periods on their own than might otherwise be the case.

All writing topics need to be close to the children's experience or concrete enough so that they are real to them. Usually, an imaginary assignment like "Write what you think Benjamin Franklin would say to his friend about Lincoln" is completely beyond them. But a preliminary discussion of the things the children like and dislike about their neighborhoods, followed by writing on the topic, which in turn is followed by a closer study of certain cooperatively determined phases of their neighborhood, can be realistic. This study can again be the subject of wide and enthusiastic writing and can be followed by a search, in the novels they are reading, for reactions (implied or expressed) of the characters in their books. Do people in books react to their neighborhoods as we have done? Such a sequence of activities is especially good with such books as Seredy's *A Tree for Peter* and Angelo's *Bells of Bleecker Street*.[8]

When the idea of children writing and even learning to *like* writing was first presented, one teacher remained silent for a long time and then exclaimed, "This is incredible! If I can get my children to write a sentence by the end of the year, I'll be happy." It took only a little time to "convince" her (and not verbally) that when children were assigned the writing of a sentence on a given unprepared, previously unconsidered topic, the stage was set for struggle. But children *will* write when there is something they can and want to say. This was an amazing young teacher, willing to try anything she saw the need for, anything that made sense to her and that she felt she could handle. The children began to write pages within a space of two weeks after this outburst, with the result that the teacher was walking on air, unable to believe her own success, trying to achieve the same results over and over again—and succeeding when the motivation was real—in order to prove to herself that this was not one of those miracles that happen only once.

One teacher used folklore as a focus for integrating all the language arts with reading. The children interviewed parents and neighbors for best-loved stories which had been handed down, and noted the place of origin. These stories were written up and discussed for similarities around the world. Then they took proverbs they knew and tallied these for content and "origin" (as far as they could trace) and tried to discover if any

[8] Kate Seredy, *A Tree for Peter* (New York: Viking Press, 1941), and Valenti Angelo, *The Bells of Bleecker Street* (New York: Viking Press, 1949).

of the stories illustrated proverbs. Following this they wrote incidents of "real life" which illustrated some of the proverbs ("Haste makes waste," "Too many cooks spoil the broth," "A stitch in time saves nine" were favorites). Then they read folklore, or tales with folklore flavor such as *The Cat Who Went to Heaven* and *Secret of the Andes* and *The White Stag,*[9] to see which proverbs seem to be the most popular among folk tales.

Something must be said at this point about the treatment of written papers when the teacher corrects them. If too much correction on all compositions is standard procedure, children soon learn that the less they write the fewer the possible mistakes, and a one-sentence paper becomes the order of the day. But this does not mean that no corrections should be made. It is true that some papers are not returned to the individual for correction—especially those that are written in confidence. There must be an invitation to write in confidence, and children must know that those confidences will never be divulged. There is more than one reason why such papers should not be returned for correction: There are guilt feelings next day when confronted with what seemed appropriate the day before; when a child writes at length, "forgetting himself," it is a shock to see the number of red marks across that paper which meant so much to him emotionally. Such papers can be "corrected" in another way: the teacher makes note of the most glaring, most typical errors, and uses this list as a basis for teaching mechanics of writing. Otherwise, the whole basic purpose of the assignment is lost. And much is also lost in relation to the child's future willingness to write. Writing should be an exciting venture. There are many ways to encourage it, and other ways to kill it.

The process of having children read each other's papers in small sociometric groups has much soundness pedagogically and psychologically. If it is agreed that the children should write each day, ways must be devised by the teacher to save himself from being overwhelmed by papers to correct. It is impossible, physically, for him to do this each day when he meets several large classes. There are not enough after-school hours in which to do this when he must also plan ahead and make some attempt at becoming acquainted with children's books. What has happened in the schools today is that teachers, feeling they must correct each paper, have cut to a bare minimum, and even less, the time devoted to writing. Children must write, and teachers must read much of what they write since we assume all writing assignments have a very real purpose, real to the teacher as well as to the children. But that does not mean laborious correcting which does the children no good—and even hurts the educational process—and certainly does not help the teacher to do a better job.

In sociometric groups, children can find each other's errors. In cases where the group is made up of children whose knowledge is so meager that they cannot distinguish between correct and incorrect construction, or cannot agree on what is correct, the teacher serves as umpire. Children can often help each other far more readily than can the teacher. When five children are reading each other's papers for content as well as for mechanical errors, five potential teachers are scrutinizing the same paper for ways in which they can help. A certain pride develops when a group can bring a paper close to "perfection" before the teacher sees it, and it is only the errors the teacher finds that "count." This prevents carping, a child's feelings being hurt because a peer criticized him, and develops a spirit of community helpfulness.

A child who writes deserves an audience. Somtimes that audience is the teacher only, especially when papers are written confidentially. Too often, the other children are the audience for thirty-five young people as they stand up and read their individual papers, one after the other—a deadening process. Children are interested in the first few that are read, but soon no one is listening and the procedure becomes mechanical. The small-group procedure eliminates this drawback and puts the responsibility for correction, for perfection, exactly where it belongs—on the children. When teachers correct constantly with too fine detail, the children become dependent on them to judge. Children should learn to take increasing responsibility for those judgments. Besides, this process is fruitful because the children are reading. Each child reads four or five papers by his classmates and scrutinizes them for two purposes.

It is surprising how quickly children learn to work in groups when they begin with short periods and are given definite tangible tasks to do which are truly group tasks and which cannot be done either individually or by the whole class. Too often the young teacher plunges into long-term committee work without giving himself and the children any previous training, without thinking through the *why* of the particular group task, without knowing the basic difference between tasks which are essentially individual and those which are truly group, and without planning the procedure step by step.

In the school situation portrayed here, where teachers or children seemed not yet ready to handle this type of set-up, sociometric twosomes, or partners, served essentially the same purpose for a time, and had the added advantage of training children to work together with one person before asking them to function in small-group activities. Here again it was the individual teacher working with his class who explored ways appropriate for him and for them and determined the goals toward which they were striving. Some teachers rarely went beyond the partner arrangement with a particular class; others gradually increased the group size for some children while they permitted certain other children to continue to work as partners; still others managed relatively early to set the "work tone" of the class in such a way that small-group work was comfortable and profitable for all; some soon learned to use both small groups and partners, whichever was most appropriate for the learning purpose.

Most teachers needed encouragement. Some were fearful of permitting thirty children to work together in fifteen teams. They were afraid of discipline problems, of a few teams "cutting up" and "spoiling it for others." These teachers had to educate themselves and the children. One did it by running a series of role-playing situations, one a day, in which two children showed how each would handle the written work of his partner. These role-playing situations were discussed by the teacher and class until the seriousness of purpose was established and both teacher and children were confident that they knew what to do. Another teacher preferred to work with one row of "double desks" (about one-third of the group) while the rest of the class occupied themselves silently reading their individually chosen books. When the teacher felt that these children knew how to proceed, he moved on to another row another day. One teacher preferred to use partner arrangements as a prestige activity, and children who could handle themselves were given the opportunity. Others had to work individually and wait for the teacher to come around so they could read to him. When such children thought they could work with another child, they informed the teacher and were promptly given an opportunity to demonstrate that ability. The responsibility was on each individual child to decide when he was ready.

The point here is that teachers, too, have individual differences. If a technique or method is psychologically and pedagogically sound, it will "work," but only when the teacher is given an opportunity to explore ways suitable and comfortable for him to make it work.

Reading Skills: Vocabulary Building and Word Recognition

Organizing reading around the common theme approach provides a "natural" for extending vocabulary without which progress in reading cannot be made but which, in turn, reading helps to expand. When children are learning to read, the vocabulary in the book must be familiar— words they know through listening, words which are meaningful experientially. Later, reading is used to increase vocabulary, to gain new experiences, to learn new words.

By and large, the children in this project worked at both levels. They were interested in materials which would bring them new experiences, but their reading levels dictated that the words, on the whole, must be known to them, except for those that were to be used for learning word-analysis skills. And these had to be few enough so that the meaning of the selection was not lost by the necessity for laboriously figuring out too many words, and so that discouragement did not set in.

Vocabulary is increased through experience. How do children learn the meaning and use of *unruly,* or *deceive,* or *floundering,* or *emphasize,* or *falter?* Teachers should use the new vocabulary in meaningful natural context, so that children become familiar with the words and what they mean before they are asked to struggle with them in a reading selection. Teachers should continue to use them at frequent intervals so that the words, and the concepts and experiences attached to them, become useful tools to the learner. This is how very young children learn language— they hear a word over and over again until they are able to attach meaning to it, until they are able to use it. It solves no problem, nor is it teaching, when a teacher uses a word once, writes it on the board, and expects children, to whom the written word is still a bewildering phenomenon, to recognize it without difficulty in the reading text. Often a story is read to children for the sole purpose of introducing words whose concepts are otherwise difficult to teach. The story provides the basic experience with the word or words, the teacher uses them meaningfully and repeatedly, and the children are encouraged to use the words as they write and speak. Taking time to build ideas creates opportunity for building vocabulary.

For example, a tape recording of a forty-minute lesson in which the teacher was introducing the project of reading to younger children reveals that he used the word "reaction" several times and that before the end of that period the children were using it as part of their own vocabularies. Here are a few excerpts from that lesson:

TEACHER: In order to get this list of little children's books as a guide for parents, we'll have to study little children's reactions to the books you read to them. For example . . .

*   *   *

TEACHER: How will you be able to tell what the little child's reaction is? If he doesn't like the book, how may he act?

•   •   •

TEACHER: In our report we'll put down the reaction of the little child. We'll say, Now there are some people who liked this book even though it didn't have a happy ending.

*　*　*

THOMAS: I agree with Mike. Probably you won't find one person that has the same reaction with [as] the child.

SANDY: If I read the same book to two children and they don't have the same reaction, what will I do?

No one method of word recognition was relied on exclusively. Children had to learn how to anticipate meaning as they read, and to use this skill as an aid in recognizing a new word. They needed, also, to be able to identify the basic word in a derivative. Basically, teachers in the project used two simple processes for reteaching skills of using context clues: One was the leading question which directed the child's thinking toward the word not recognized in order to help him find "clues."[10] Does the story take place at night or in the daytime? What does Susie want for a birthday present? Another way was to have the child skip the bothersome word and continue to read to the end of the sentence, returning to the word to see if context helped. Teachers helped the whole class to discover how to do this for themselves and for others. If one child asked another for help, the second child asked a question connecting the unknown with a clue to guide him, or he urged him to read to the end of the sentence, skipping the word temporarily and returning to it when he had the complete thought. It was necessary for some children to have these processes emphasized daily, for only when all the children knew what was being done, and why, could assistance be given. Being able to verbalize, to intellectualize the processes and the reasons, not only helped the child who asked for aid, but the child who was giving it, for there were many times when he too needed help with the same skill. Most important of all, children began to feel that they were *learning how to learn,* that they could attack the problem intelligently.

Another process which was taught was in one sense a part of the process of using context clues. In another sense, it served as motivation to go on in spite of difficulty and also as a check on the children's comprehension. It served to emphasize comprehension as a basic feature of vocabulary building. It was the process of predicting events. What do you think is going to happen? To answer this intelligently, one must have understood what went before, and this would provide a focus for more intelligent reading of what was to follow. This was emphasized in almost every

[10] For one type of lesson plan, on context clues, see Chapter 3.

reading session in which common skills were taught to all, and in which common reading materials were used.

Once the child had learned the vocabulary, he needed opportunities to hear the words, to see them, to use them in a variety of different situations. The teacher continued to use the words in a natural way at intervals which were first short, then longer. These words appeared frequently —perhaps in the written directions teachers gave to children. The day after the children read their stories to siblings, the teacher wrote on the board, "Describe the reaction of your child to the book you read." This whole process of providing sufficient experiences necessary for vocabulary building, of using new words in a variety of situations, of using the context to help figure them out, was facilitated by the theme approach of teaching reading. Who plays the *role* of *arbiter* in your family? Do different people play different roles? There are *arbiters* in books too, in books about families and about teen-agers, and children can watch for situations in which people *arbitrate* at home or in school or among peers. The point is that the children must be enabled to build a substantial vocabulary around areas that are allowed sufficient time for study, and which include consideration of ideas requiring a particular vocabulary for their expression.

Phonics, as a method of teaching word-analysis skills, has made the headlines for the past few years—to such an extent that it is difficult for teachers to view phonetic analysis objectively. When it is viewed objectively it is seen as one of several procedures used to help a child with word recognition and analysis. To teach through this method, using isolated words, bears little fruit for several reasons: (1) The children's chief difficulty is reading for meaning, reading to find out what someone else is saying to them. Learning phonetic analysis through isolated words only increases the lack of meaning reading holds for the child. (2) The children have not yet learned that reading can be a pleasurable experience. Learning in this way only strengthens the frustration of their earlier sad experiences with the reading process. (3) Teachers often find that many of the children who are still having difficulty with reading have already "had" this method. It did little for them then, and emphasis on it is not likely to improve the situation now.

Other aids to word recognition must come first: context clues, for example. Then phonetic analysis can be used in meaningful context as the child is grappling with a word. Teachers in this project taught phonetic analysis only after they knew that the child was reading fluently and with meaning. Unfortunately, the children who seemed to need phonetic analysis most could not profit from it, even at junior high school age, when more children can use this method than could previously. It took a certain degree of mental maturity to *see* the similarity of *sound* on the printed page. Teachers did not find necessary a highly complicated and intricate method of teaching phonetic analysis. They simply used it as needed to help a child who was "stuck" as he read, and made sure that the whole word was kept intact, that letters were not sounded in isolation. For example, if a child failed to recognize the word *smudge* and did not even attempt to attack the initial sound, the teacher helped him arrive at the meaning from the context. Once the meaning was clearly established they read together to a point in the story at which it was reasonable to stop, and then went back to the troublesome word. The teacher isolated the whole word from its sentence, writing it on a piece of paper (or on a 3 x 5 card so the child could file it for future reference). He mentioned several known words beginning with *sm:* smell, small, smoke, smile. When the *sm* sound—as it is seen in print—was clearly established, the child was helped to get the next part of the word: *smudge* is like *smell* in the way it begins, but in the latter part it is like *fudge* or *judge*.

None of this drill or teaching of a "new" skill was undertaken while the child was reading in an audience situation. It was when he was reading to the teacher alone, or to his partner, or when he asked for help during silent reading periods, that most of such instruction was given.

As a child gained in his ability to figure out words for himself, and as the teacher gained in resourcefulness in finding materials suited to each child's ability, there was much less need for teaching new words before reading a common selection. The reading activity began to be used for learning new words.

Teachers used very few different types of written drills and exercises; it was not necessary to burden them with the task of learning about a great variety of drills or with devising ways to implement them. Nor did they feel such drills were particularly useful for the children. They did use a very few, only on occasion, only for a very specific purpose, and only for a few selected children. One was for the purpose of helping children distinguish between words that were giving them difficulty, words such as *then* and *than, where* and *when, whom* and *what*. For this the teachers prepared a list of phrases using the vocabulary the children had already learned, and asked them to circle, for each phrase, the correct word that followed.

working in the laboratory	Where	When
after the busy season	Where	When
during the recess period	Where	When

The teachers spent some time on syllabication, stressing the division of words according to sound rather than following the dictionary. They realized that there is difference of opinion among lexicographers as to exactly how some words should be divided. Previously, they had followed the practice of having the children look up every word in the dictionary—a time-consuming procedure. Teachers realized that there is a hierarchy of values when the school day is limited. Some words were checked; the dictionary was not a forgotten tool. But first things must come first. In all cases, the words used were those encountered in current reading material.

Teachers found value in the use of "cut-up stories" to be reassembled. They worked with the children, helping them discover the transitions from paragraph to paragraph. These stories were mounted on cards, paragraph by paragraph (sometimes two or three paragraphs on one card to make it easier for the children to succeed in this task), and the children put them together into a sequential story.

In all cases, stories were in the context of the theme under consideration and used the vocabulary necessary for that consideration. Stories were obtained from discarded books and from *Practical English* (a weekly published by Scholastic Magazines, Inc.); some of the stories used had been written by classes of children who were more verbal. Interest in this activity was as high as if it had been a picture puzzle.

Nor were teachers averse to using *Classic Comics*. Some of these were quite appropriate to discussions at hand, had high interest value, and repeated words often enough for children to learn to recognize them. When a small group of children in one class obtained the *Classic Comic*, "The Magic Fountain," interest reached a peak. Some of the children played the parts of the characters while others read the explanations and setting. The teacher reported that "they followed the text eagerly; when one hesitated, the other one helped him. They attacked words as a team." Here, figuring out words and written ideas became a group project about which children could actually become excited.

Spelling

Even spelling was taught in such a way as to aid with word recognition in reading and with vocabulary extension. The city-wide spelling list was used more to satisfy the teachers than for any other reason, because the list was largely in isolation and had little connection with the content teachers and children were considering. There were spelling lists from other sources which were given even greater attention: an individual list drawn from the words the child really tried to use in his writing, and a composite list made up of words that were commonly misspelled in the children's written work.

The children were told, even encouraged, to indicate their need for help whenever they felt they could not spell a word properly. It was explained to them that seeing the word written incorrectly made it more difficult to "unlearn" than if it were set down correctly to begin with. Also, they were led to believe that recognition of the fact that they could not spell a word was a step forward. When a child raised his hand for help, the teacher went to him immediately with a 3 x 5 slip of paper or card and wrote the word on it in large letters. The child copied it and continued to write. When his piece of writing was completed he wrote the word three times from memory, each time covering what he had written.

The teacher had previously taught the children how to learn to spell. Visual memory was stressed. They must not look at a copy of the word while they wrote. They could look carefully, all they wanted to, at the word before they wrote, but when they wrote, the word must not be in sight. Most of these children had a history of having copied words twenty-five times, without learning to spell them. They did not need to. There was the word above to look at each time they wrote it. Most of the children had a common difficulty in reading. They failed to note details. They could note them as they copied them but that is where the noting ended. Now they had a copy of the word enlarged so that details stood out. Now they studied the word before writing and noted the details carefully enough to carry them in their "mind's eye." Spelling "out loud" was discouraged; visual memory, necessary in spelling correctly, was encouraged.

Since the words were those that children used frequently, and since the content of what they were writing was correlated with what they were discussing and reading, this method fortified word recognition in reading. After a very few weeks, it became evident that children were making a start at noting details, noting differences between *where* and *were, thimble* and *thistle.*

Grammar and Usage

Grammar and usage were also taught with indirect focus on strengthening word recognition. Teachers used the method of building up sentences instead of the usual tearing down. For example, the teacher (or children) named an action word, let us say "crawls," and the children thought of as many things that crawl as they could. Then the order was reversed, and a noun was named—"automobile." The children listed as many verbs as they could, describing what an automobile does. Thus, they not only gained the basic feeling for how a sentence is created, but the verb or the noun—*crawl* and later *automobile*—which was to remain constant while they created the other part of sentence, was a word which needed reinforcement for reading, either because of word-attack skills or word recognition.

The process was continued as time went on, never reverting to sentence analysis, but always using the creating process of building sentences, always keeping one element or one part of speech constant. It was this constancy which gave the opportunity for teaching reading skills and vocabulary and usage. If children confused *lie* and *lay*, these became the constants. The children were called upon to change the rest of the sentence; they now had an opportunity to truly learn the difference.

Later, the adverb and adjective were introduced by keeping the noun and verb constant and changing first one modifier and then the other. Even clauses were taught this way, and difficulties with sentence structure remedied. For example, if children wrote *Because I went home* and called this a sentence, it was difficult to explain by rules why it is not. But if *Because I went home* was kept as the constant clause and the teacher called for another clause which finished its meaning, which told exactly what happened when you went home, it was much less difficult to teach independent and dependent clauses. The children were in the meantime creating new ideas, learning to recognize whatever words were consciously used by the teacher over and over again.

Teachers were not concerned with whether these particular children could name each part of speech; they were concerned with their writing creatively and meaningfully and accurately. They were concerned with having all procedures used fortify the children's reading skills. Yet it is interesting to note that children learned more about the names of the parts of speech than teachers had hoped they would. This occurred only in cases where teachers gave them an opportunity to show what they knew through the building process. When the test consisted of a sentence already created by someone else, and required the children to name the parts of speech of the various words, they were at a loss. But then, so were the others who had been taught by the method of parsing.

Oral Reading

The basic procedure of using a constant theme approach to individualizing the work gave opportunities for still other practices, too, practices of extreme importance in strengthening the children's reading ability.

For example, it offered opportunities for teachers to find occasions for oral reading. They realized that oral reading should continue to be an important part of the program, even though silent reading predominated.

Because most children read well by the time they reach junior high school, teachers often tend to forget the role played by oral reading in the process of learning to read. It is through oral reading that a teacher can diagnose a child's difficulties; it is through this process that children are motivated to read better, to practice their reading beforehand. This does not mean that each child should be asked or even permitted to stumble through a passage with thirty-five peers as audience. Audience situations can be provided in other ways. There are, again, the small sociometric groupings which can serve the purpose. There are times when children can share something with only one other classmate. This became evident in one routine procedure which teachers found very fruitful—the use of the first five minutes of every core session for oral reading in "duets." Each child had an outside reading book on his own level, whether it was on the Westward Movement or fantasies for young children or an adventure story. In the adventure-story sequence children were trying to come to some conclusion about what constituted adventure. Did you have to risk your life? Was there adventure in every-day life? Was the same experience adventure for everyone? A standard homework assignment was reading from that book every night. Each child had a mimeographed chart on which he made certain entries (see page 42).

Then he prepared the paragraph he liked best for reading to his classmate. After reading to his classmate he entered two or three words in the proper column, words he would like to be able to recognize more readily. This work was begun as soon as the children entered the classroom, even while the teacher was on hall duty. Any questions were referred to the teacher. As soon as the teacher returned he circulated around the room, listening, advising, noting progress, making comments of encouragement on the charts wherever this was warranted. In other words, at the start of each day, every child had a chance to read aloud and be heard, and the time consumed was only five minutes.

Teachers frequently used plays for oral reading. For example, there was *Seeing the Elephant*[11] by Dan Totheroh when they were studying the Westward Movement, or scenes from *I Remember Mama*[12] when they

[11] Dan Totheroh, *Seeing the Elephant* (New York: Dramatic Play Service, 1939). This play was one of the America in Action Series of one-act plays for young people.

[12] John Van Druten, *I Remember Mama*, in *Three Comedies of American Family Life*, edited by Joseph Mersand (New York: Washington Square Press, Inc., 1961).

READING PROGRESS SHEET

NAME _____ CORE TEACHER _____ CLASS _____

Date	Title of book	Time begun Page begun	Time ended Page ended	Minutes per page	Words for practice	Most exciting part or part I liked	Teacher's comments

were considering what children learn from families. There were several short plays in earlier issues of *Practical English* which teachers saved for this kind of use. Since these were common readings, they were not given to children to struggle with alone. Always the teacher worked with them, even to the extent of first reading it to them while children watched their books. Soon they lost their self-consciousness about reading aloud and everyone wanted to read at sight. In all cases, teachers had to hold out for silent preparation beforehand, for it was in the motivated practice of these materials that children developed their skills.

Much work was also done with choral reading of poetry. It was necessary to use simple uncomplicated poems, for the sentence structure in poetry is not easy for children who are poor readers. But "Casey at the Bat," done in chorus, was always a "big seller" as were ballads and many other pieces of poetry. This method of choral reading provided motivation for rereading many times until words were recognized in the natural course of events. The teacher did a good deal of reading aloud so that the children could see and hear him express an emotion which was aroused by words on a cold printed page. In addition it was through his oral reading that a teacher could introduce the children to many new books, open up new vistas and new ideas. The children still needed models for good reading, and most of them had no source other than their own teacher. As the children watched the teacher enjoy reading, they began to sense that people derive pleasure from this thing which caused them so much difficulty. Also, there was a community of feeling when the teacher read to them. It was good for children to feel this closeness—connected with books—with other human beings. Some children had experienced it in their early years when their parents read to them; others had probably never experienced it until they entered school. Now there was anticipation of pleasant relationships with teacher and classmates whenever the teacher picked up a book to read to them. This atmosphere was important in changing the children's attitudes toward books.

The tape recorder has numerous ramifications and unending possibilities for oral reading. Its motivational powers are unquestioned. Children will practice and practice untiringly, without a murmur, in order to perfect a passage for the recorder. It is an excellent device for showing children how much they have improved in ten weeks, let us say, and thus it can provide further motivation at a time when interest lags or the tasks involved in learning to read become difficult. It is also a way of taking care of individual and small-group problems: The teacher (or some more advanced member of the group) reads a story onto the tape for children who are still on a considerably lower level. These children work alone later, listening to the tape and at the same time watching the book (one with which they would be unable to cope without such assistance). Then they try reading it without the tape, noting the words at which they are blocked. They may play the tape as many times as they feel necessary. The words they do not know furnish material for work with word-attack skills.

When the children themselves feel that they have improved, they ask the teacher for a special hearing or for an extra chance to use the tape for recording their progress. It is their responsibility to know when they are improving, to know when they've gotten "that certain feeling." The teacher also encourages each member of the class to observe the progress made by the partner with whom he does his daily five-minute reading and to encourage him to demonstrate that progress.

Plans must also be made within the context of work organized around a common theme and around certain concepts related to it to create opportunities for rereading many selections. Each rereading should be done for a different purpose. This does not affect work with the individual books the children are reading, but applies to the common stories and plays. The use of plays and choral reading of poems, and the high motivation they offer for reading, have already been discussed. Motivation for rereading stories has to be planned, too. Children need to understand the reason for rereading both in terms of their own skill building and in terms of the function the reading activity will serve. A function already considered is reading to younger children. There are many devices that are fruitful, each according to the story itself and the needs of the class. For example, with the "Tell-Tale Heart"[13] by Poe, which may have to be read in good measure by the teacher, only simple questions are needed as motivation for rereading because the story is a gripping one—such questions as: When do you first become aware that this man is insane? What are the other places where Poe makes you more and more sure that this is a madman?

There are usually differences of opinion which become evident as they are aired in the ensuing discussion, and this provides the motivation for a partial third reading. Who is right? How do you know? Prove your point with evidence from the story.

Other stories require different types of motivation for rereading. For example, "Ski-High,"[14] by B. J. Chute, is fun to read as if it were a play.

[13] In Rewey B. Inglis, *Adventures in American Literature* (New York: Harcourt, Brace and World, Inc., 1952).

[14] In Frances T. Humphreville and Frances S. Fitzgerald, *Top Flight* (Chicago: Scott, Foresman and Company, 1961).

So the children reread to decide how many scenes there will be, and exactly where each will begin and end. When everyone has made his own individual judgment, a discussion follows to resolve the differences, and a partial third reading is achieved when children are asked to present "proof."

Another group of stories lends itself best to reading up to the climax, after which the children write the endings. Then the "real" ending is read, followed by the reading of a few created by the children. A discussion follows along these lines: "Some of you have happy endings; others sad. Why did you choose that kind?" Children are asked to give particulars from the story itself—a rereading process. "The author did not mean that the ending could be anything at all—either happy or sad. He gave you cues all along. Can you find them?" Stories suitable for such analysis are Leonard Ross's "Cemetery Path"[15] and Guy De Maupassant's "The Necklace."[16]

USING COMMON READINGS

Striving for an individualized approach in order to ensure each child's equal opportunity to learn need not bar common readings. Common readings offer common experiences that are of utmost importance to group life, to group understandings, to group feelings of belonging. Through common readings the teacher has the opportunity to introduce children to fine pieces of literature; this is one of the important uses of class time. Even though the children cannot handle such materials alone, they still have the right to be introduced to superior pieces of literature. And since the teacher is assisting, there is no question about wide reading ranges at this point. Even the junior high school child who does not yet read at second-grade level can enjoy and profit from hearing and participating in discussion of such a piece. He need not be deprived. For the rereading he may sit with a partner who is glancing through the story again to find evidence of insanity, for instance. He watches as his partner does this, discussing what he is selecting and why. Surprisingly enough, it is not long before the poorest reader makes some contribution to the performance.

[15] In Matilda Bailey and Ullin W. Leavell, *Worlds To Explore* (New York: American Book Company, 1951).

[16] In M. E. Speare, *The Pocket Book of Short Stories* (New York: Pocket Books, Inc., 1941).

SUMMARY

As a result of this unified procedure of teaching skills and content, and also as a result of the individualized reading program which was a part of it, remarkable growth took place. The understanding of children which teachers gained, the way in which they used those understandings, and the warm accepting interactions were contributing factors. Some evidences of this growth are given in this chapter, but it is important to offer a word of caution. No teacher ever learned to use all the procedures described here all at once. Each teacher had to select those elements which he felt he could work through at one time successfully. When he had tried and found fruitful the process of introducing several books to children until each child had a book of his own on his own level and around a particular topic, *then* perhaps the teacher tried pairing children as partners so that more oral reading could be done. When this was going smoothly, he perhaps chose another procedure to perfect. He did not do this all in one year. One teacher chose to work through the project of reading to young siblings; another teacher at that time preferred to practice how to develop certain word-attack skills he felt the children needed. But in all cases, teachers were encouraged to learn new processes and gain new understandings as soon as they had mastered the old ones.

As the project progressed, there was a feeling of excitement and adventure on the part of the teachers who did the work. It is true that what is described in this pamphlet happened in a unique school, unique in the sense that the personnel of the college and the junior high school staff really did work *together* on common problems, with mutual respect and with mutual benefit. But it does not require outside "agents" such as college personnel to stimulate the kinds of activities and attitudes that were developed. It is possible to keep this feeling of excitement about teaching and learning throughout a life-long professional career. Teachers can do it for each other. Any two or three teachers can come together to try to find out how to do something better than they have been doing it. Here lies the groundwork for professional adventure. Here, too, is a role for the professional administrator—to help such activity find ground roots, to support it, to nourish it, to keep it growing.

3 • Planning and Preparation

THERE ARE SEVERAL AREAS OF PLANNING AND PREPARATION WHICH A
teacher must consider in order to ensure that children do grow in reading.
One area deals with getting to know children, another with understanding
children's motivations to learn; a third, with planning curriculum adjustments; a fourth, with planning daily lessons; and a fifth, with finding
suitable materials.

GETTING TO KNOW CHILDREN

Some elements had to be planned before the teacher ever met the
class; other equally important aspects, such as diagnosing, had to be done
as an integral part of the reading program. Some lent themselves to preplanning as well as to further and continuous diagnosis which in turn led
to more intelligent planning. For example, the area of getting to know
children required that teachers understand the mental health condition of
the children and the need for improving it.

There were many pieces of evidence that the program needed to stress
mental health improvement along with the reading program. Typically,
the records from the elementary school read thus:

Attended four elementary schools before this one. Constant behavior
problem. Fights with classmates.

Seems unhappy; doesn't get along well with others.

Very sensitive. Needs praise. Difficulties with certain vowel combina-
tions: *voice, noise, text, next.*

Lisp.

Mouth breather; frequent colds.

Stutters, attends speech class.

Very poor attendance record.

Emotional, social behavior problems; nervous habits; mechanical ability; doesn't get along with classmates; doesn't get along with sister.

INTERVIEW: Mother said child seemed disturbed and indifferent. Two YEARS LATER: Mother and child are attending clinic. Unable to express himself in writing.

Record of being shy, withdrawn. Needs encouragement and direction. Usually lethargic.

Ward of Sheltering Arms Children's Service. Was started in a preprimer in grade 6. At first, refused to read; attends special reading class.

Poor background. Language problem. Belittles her own ability.

Thus, out of a class of thirty, two children's records contained positive statements like "interested in art"; twelve were those quoted above; one read, "Transferred from parochial school; few records available"; and the rest had no comment at all.

When teachers considered these records carefully and connected them with what they already knew from psychology courses and case studies, they realized that every procedure they planned to use should have a positive effect on the mental health of the children, and that this in turn would affect the efficiency with which the children would be able to learn. Every one of the classroom procedures used had its roots in a deep concern for this aspect of a child's life. For example, the stress on early success experiences and the procedures adopted for this purpose were a direct outgrowth of that concern. Teachers were not expected to be therapists, but they were helped to understand and use sound psychological principles, so that learning would be facilitated. When children felt the glow of achievement this would boost their feelings of self-respect and self-worth, and this in turn would bring about better mental health conditions.

Very early in the first semester two or three diagnostic procedures were used. One was the administration of SRA intelligence tests (SRA Non-verbal Form, published by Science Research Associates, Chicago, 1947), not because another test was needed, but because children usually scored higher on this nonverbal test than on the Pintner, for instance. The new scores gave the teachers a feeling that these children were within the sphere of their assistance. Teachers could see that intelligence involved more than one factor, some of which might not be measured by the verbal intelligence test usually administered. This awareness helped teachers to be mindful of planning activities which could develop multifaceted abilities, and which could appeal to children on various levels in order to give them a number of avenues along which to further their learnings.

The second instrument was the sociogram which helped teachers know where to focus their attention and how to gain preliminary clues about possible causes of difficulties. Teachers were given clues to the identification of the children who were having personal difficulties with other children so that the relationship between these and reading difficulties could be studied. The results of children's choices were used in pairing children for reading partners or for small reading groups.[1] Teachers could see that the children whom nobody had chosen as a companion tended to feel uncomfortable if asked to read aloud in a large group. They could see the importance of creating a climate in which every child, even those who were unwanted, could learn. For this reason, some "partnerships" had to consist of three rather than two children. This was true in cases where an unchosen child was paired with a child who also needed to be satisfied by being paired with a chosen partner.

Some teachers gave a questionnaire similar to the *Van Pit Series, Wishes*[2] in order to learn some of the kinds of problems with which children had to contend. The concern was not with statistical test validity, only with ways of helping teachers know the mental health impact on these children of the struggle to learn. In one class, a high proportion of the children expressed a need for self-respect (one of the "wishes" tested) and an item-analysis helped teachers see a little of what this meant to the child. This awareness bore directly on plans for teaching reading: All procedures used must build up the feelings of self-worth of the children. For example, teachers planned to help children make choices and to help them see that the teacher respected those choices. They asked: What book will you read? How many pages can you manage? What questions would the class like to consider first? What do children think of this or that part of the story?

In the first weeks of the first semester, the teacher asked the children (after appropriate motivation in each case) to write about himself in various contexts: "The Things That Bother Me Most," "Stories My Parents

---

[1] For more detailed uses of the sociogram in other situations see Hilda Taba and Deborah Elkins, *With Focus on Human Relations* (Washington, D.C.: American Council on Education, 1950).

[2] The original *Van Pit Series* is no longer available but the instrument was based on "forced choice," the child being forced to choose those items which were most applicable and those least applicable to his life "when he was younger." For example, "When you were younger, which one of these wishes would you have wanted most? Put an M in front of that one. Which one was least important to you? Put an L in front of it.
1. I used to wish I had other children to play with.
2. I used to wish people wouldn't yell at me so much.
3. I used to wish teachers would be pleased with my work.
4. I used to wish I knew what I wanted to be."

Like to Tell About Me," "Why I'd Like (Wouldn't Like) to Move."[3] From even a cursory study of these papers, teachers obtained many ideas of what was important to children. They saw some of the specific areas in which experiences tended to affect mental health positively or negatively. They gained a picture of pressures in some homes to produce high marks in reading and other school work, of the child's concern about his achievement, of aspirations and ambitions too unrealistic or virtually nonexistent. Each of these things bore directly on the mental health of the child. Awareness of the specifics was necessary to further intelligent planning. These kinds of writing assignments played a role all through the two grades and were an integral part of the curriculum. As the teacher discovered new facts about each child, he could handle his relationship with him more intelligently and could plan the learning experiences more insightfully.

Getting to know children meant a knowledge of their interests, too. Just talking with children about many things gave a wealth of clues. This was done systematically as well as spontaneously by taking advantage of the choice bits of motivational occasions that arose. Writing helped, too. Every paper that children wrote, if the topics were thoughtfully chosen with this purpose in mind, helped the teacher discover much about the child. For example: "Meet My Family," "Things I Like to Do," "Things I Hate to Do," "My Three Wishes," "My Worries"—all were most revealing. It must be said here, however, that as with topics previously listed much depended on the relationship of the children with the teacher. If it was warm and "giving," the children were relatively uninhibited in what they said and wrote; if it was cold and restricting, mere words and few were the result.

An important point is that this finding-out process can be and was an integral part of teaching procedures, of implementing the curriculum. Teachers worry so much about time that it is necessary to offer diagnostic procedures which at the same time are "teaching" procedures, so that they cannot reject the finding-out process on the basis that the time is not available. Also, these procedures can be the basis of good learning experiences. Children need to write; writing about what they know is necessary.

Let us consider the matter of discovering what children are doing with their time outside of school. What do they do when they are free to choose for themselves? Two-day accounts of after-school activities, kept at intervals from the close of school to suppertime and then from suppertime to bedtime, can be a real eye-opener. Besides the information they offer,

[3] For further suggestions on diagnosis see Hilda Taba, *Diagnosing Human Relations Needs* (Washington, D.C.: American Council on Education, 1951).

they also provide other good writing experiences. Usually, if not confidential, these can be read in small sociometric groups and tallied by the children according to certain categories. How many of us have active interests and activities? How many of us spend a large portion of our time watching television? What is a too-large portion? This kind of activity, during which the children study the data to discover something about themselves, is a fruitful one for discussions, for further reading, and for writing. Did anyone go to a library of his own accord? Did anyone pick up a newspaper or book of his own accord? What did people talk about when they could choose anything in the world they wanted? Are the subjects we talk about wide in range? How do people find new things to talk about? The wealth of possibilities in this type of activity is apparent. The writing assignment itself must be carried on in school. It is too difficult for the children to manage alone.

It is after the children study themselves that the teacher can make his own study for whatever he is seeking. Who supervises children's activities? Which children seem to be completely alone? With whom do they communicate? About what?

Finding children's interests can be done in other ways, too, ways that are more prosaic perhaps, and not fruitful enough to serve as the sole fact-finding technique, but nevertheless useful. A list of book titles, which sample a variety of interests, may be presented to the children to mark which ones they would like to read if they could find such a book (the titles are not necessarily real ones) and which ones hold no interest for them at all.[4] Children can have wonderful discussions of inventories that are administered and they can add titles and areas which they feel are grossly neglected.

UNDERSTANDING CHILDREN'S MOTIVATIONS
TO LEARN

When teachers tried to find out about the children and the children's interests, it was primarily toward the end that they might gain an understanding of the factors which motivate children to learn. These factors needed to be known by those who were guiding that learning.

A glance through the chapter on procedures (see pages 4–46) will bring to light the many ways in which the things that were done in the

---

[4] For a sample of such a list see Albert J. Harris, *How to Increase Reading Ability* (New York: Longmans, Green and Company, 1961), p. 481.

classroom relied heavily on such understanding of the factors which motivated the children.

One class chose "teen-age problems" as their topic area around which to read. Much excitement was created as well as real motivation for several children to read one book. This was so because they set up a structure by which a panel would present the major problem posed by a book and the audience was invited to tell what they would do about it. Then, the "solution" was given as described by the author. This caused much heated discussion because in many instances children rejected the author's solution as unrealistic and not a true solution. The motivation here was on different levels: activity with peers, participation in the selection of their own topic which from the beginning meant something was at stake for each of them, and a chance to pit their wits against the author and to demonstrate that their experiences "counted" too.

When the teacher permitted children to choose "teen-age problems" as a reading topic and then created panel-audience situations in which children evaluated the author's solution, it was evident that the teacher had studied and learned much about the children. He knew that the children were striving for independence and that giving them opportunities to say authors do or do not know what they are talking about when they pose solutions was a realistic recognition of what motivated children. This teacher knew, too, from many diagnostic techniques, that a number of children needed to be accepted by their peers and to function in groups and to extend their contacts. Thus, the procedure here described gave some opportunity to meet another need. And the very act of permitting children to *choose* (not from thin air but after a number of stimulating experiences such as stories, discussions, newspaper articles) helped meet the need for self-regard and for influencing other people and their own environment. Here was a demonstration of the way a teacher planned to provide a variety of purposes and satisfactions in the learning process, since no one set of procedures could motivate all children at all times.

Will children choose the same topic, year after year, as some teachers fear? The answer is usually *no*. It depends on the criteria set for the choice. If one criterion is that the topic to be studied must not have been studied recently, that eliminates it. Some groups never choose teen-age problems as a topic for consideration, but prefer adventure or courage. Teachers ought not to fear the possibility of children's repeated choice of a topic anyway. Many concepts and much content can be covered in such a study area, and if children feel the need for reconsidering it another year, new ideas and materials are ample.

One teacher used ownership as a motivating force. Many of the children had never owned a "real" book. She introduced several attractively produced pocketbook editions of stories and helped children become intrigued about the prospect of ownership. There was no difficulty getting most of the twenty-five-cent pieces after they made their selection from the sample set. Each day the teacher was greeted with "Did they come in yet?" At first there was a problem of getting them interested in other books while they waited, but before long, committees began to go to the public library to return with several books for themselves and others. And now began the trek of books from homes to school. Somehow, the children in one teacher's class of better readers became aware of the need for books that were not too difficult, and soon books they had read some time ago, and which were now outgrown to a degree, began to appear around the room. Their names were in them. Children in this section knew those names, and the "takers" were many. Here again, the motivation to do what status-peers do is strong.

There were some disappointments when the pocket books arrived, though general happiness reigned. For example, one child had selected *Party Perfect*[5] by Gay Head even though the teacher had cautioned her that this was not a story book. When she discovered the truth of the matter for herself, there was great unhappiness—but not for long. Since most book distributors offer discounts on large orders and since children paid full retail price for the books, there was money left to purchase a few extra titles, with the full agreement of the children. There was, therefore, a small but varied assortment of extras so that a quick exchange could be made for the child whose purchase was not pleasing to her.

This teacher was astonished to see a number of children read half a book in a little over half a week. When the books arrived, and after the excitement died down, the full class period was devoted to reading quietly. The teacher, by now familiar with individual aptitudes, spent her time reading in turn with those children who were unable to handle their books alone. She had permitted them to buy ones she knew might give trouble. This quiet period turned out to be such a valuable one that the teacher planned occasions for other similar periods. Since children had a chance in school time to become involved in their books, some took them home voluntarily and read a goodly amount at night. It was valuable, too, because she had a tension-less period (since all other children were engrossed) to give real help to individuals who needed it.

In such periods, when one child finished his own book, he took time to catch up in a slower child's book and then read with him quietly off in

[5] Published by Scholastic Book Services (a division of Scholastic Magazines, Inc.), Englewood Cliffs, N. J.

a corner of the room, so that he, too, could finish his book more quickly. The children learned to read *with* their partners, not always *to* them.

Soon the children "saw the sense" in the reading progress chart (see page 42). They could use their summary sentence to remind them of the content when they wanted to tell about particular events or people. And there was very high interest in adding the number of minutes recorded and dividing to find out how many minutes per page on the average for the first book. Then they compared that average with the second one, provided the book was comparable in format. Here the incentive was seeing one's own improvement, making greater progress. Incidentally, it was through this process that many children, for the first time, began to understand the meaning of "average" and the process of finding an average.

Going to the public library with the teacher once or twice a week after school, to browse, became accepted practice for one classroom. Rarely did less than six children voluntarily accompany her each time, and sometimes there were more. This does not mean that all the children had a consuming interest in reading. It does mean that the teacher played an important role in making going to the library and reading a "habit," even though, at first, they went only for the fun of accompanying her.

Soon the children began to bring in books for each other as they came to know the interests of their peers. More and more frequent library trips were made, usually in small groups. One small group went on Monday and brought back books for themselves and others who requested such service. Another day a second group made the trip.

Teachers knew, too, that children's aspiration levels were based on previous experiences. Continuous failure tended to bring about low levels of aspiration, as the children came to expect less of themselves. Therefore, success experiences were a part of motivation to achieve more. It was a question not of providing one success experience but a long sequence of such experiences to offset the effects of previous failure. That was the reason for concentrating on projects involving little children's books, for making sure children had available books on their own reading level.

Testing also served as motivation for the child to give greater effort to his reading. For this purpose, a simple "device" like the McCall-Crabbs *Standard Test Lessons in Reading*[6] served. Children corrected their own work and kept their own scores. They knew they must put forth some effort in between test dates if improvement was to be apparent.

---

[6] William A. McCall and Lelah Mae Crabbs, *Standard Test Lessons in Reading* (New York: Teachers College Press, Teachers College, Columbia University, 1961).

(Testing, therefore, should not be too frequent.) There was a hazard in this process: Some children became emotionally upset when they realized that they were so far below grade. Real setbacks occurred. The teacher had to be ready to encourage, reassure, and offer special tangible help to those youngsters.

The teacher's knowledge of what motivates children to learn and of how to plan procedures had positive effects. This was evident on one occasion when the children told the school newspaper "reporters" that their class reading chart was the most interesting thing they were doing.

PLANNING CURRICULUM ADJUSTMENTS

Once the teacher has some knowledge about the children as learners, it is necessary to plan curriculum adjustments. When the whole school operates within the framework of an existing course of study, the children need to feel a part of that whole. They compare notes with peers in other classes, which, at first sight, may make it seem difficult to achieve the necessary curriculum adjustments. Children soon find that "everybody else is studying The Westward Movement. Why don't we?" A course of study need not be inflexible. Much that the children need can be achieved under the topic of The Westward Movement, once the teacher really knows what those needs are. In other words, the large area of study can often be followed with a complete modification of details of procedure and of content and materials. Wherever the large area of study can be maintained, and still serve the needs of these children, it should be. The children are not so retarded that they do not know what is going on about them. They are sensitive to being excluded in any way. The fact that they are called a nonlanguage group, meaning that they are not permitted to study a foreign language, has been the cause of much hurt feeling, great sensitivity, and many feelings of inferiority and antagonism. There is no reason why these children cannot learn a few phrases and sentences of a foreign language in the same way they learned English, by rote. A substantial amount of time need not be spent on this when there are other more important needs to be satisfied, but a teacher can say *good morning* and *good work!* in Spanish as well as in English, and give the children an opportunity to feel included in the offerings available to others.

Another important factor with respect to the course of study is the teacher. Young teachers, as mentioned earlier, need a feeling of security. Building a curriculum alone, without the strength gained from one's fellows, is not easy. To be guided at least by broad areas of content gives a measure of safety.

Even though the course of study was spelled out by the board of education, it was possible to use it in such a way as to permit and even to encourage children to learn and to meet the children's needs and abilities as described above. For example, the social studies curriculum guide called for a study of the child's immediate community which included home, school, and neighborhood. This offered many appropriate possibilities for experiences for the children which would assist them as they read. *Family* has already been mentioned as a topic in Chapter 2. The topic suggested a multitude of concepts to be developed: The family is the first place where children receive an education. Families teach children many things they need to know. Families today have to face some problems which are new. Teen-agers have problems and responsibilities in family life. Concepts such as these were already of real interest or concern to the children, or carried a potential for high interest. For example, although no child had thought of his family as an educational institution, the idea captured attention immediately because the reaction to it was either positive or negative. This quick expression of interest could have been anticipated from what teachers knew about the children—they were struggling for independence but there remained strong feelings of dependence and an equally strong need to have the world recognize *their* families despite the relatively poor achievement of the offspring.

The topic provided a framework for reading and discussion and writing, and a large number of ideas around which reading could be focused, and experiences—vicarious and real—could be built. When children interviewed parents or adult relatives about their hopes and aspirations for themselves, this in itself was an experience, for many of them had long since stopped talking to parents about things that really counted. And when they returned to school with collected data, a whole series of new experiences could be planned: tallying items, studying them, discussing them, writing up interviews to be used later for comparative purposes, talking to each other about what all this meant, reading their books with new insights and for new ideas.

Teachers were not interested only in the mechanics of reading; mechanics are tools to the reading process, which is essentially a thought process. Children gain ideas when they really read, but they must also have ideas to bring to that reading. Ideas can be gained only through experiences. Experiences can come through books as well as through the process of daily living. The ideas gained by having "lived through" one book can be used to enrich the reading of the next.

Another topic in the course of study was the historical development of the city. A very limited amount of time was devoted to this in comparison to that given to the previous topic. One teacher handled it through short biographical vignettes which he read to the children. Some of these were rewritten by him from text material or by another more academically capable class, and then mimeographed. In one instance the children in another class of greater academic ability, but assigned to this same teacher, made up a play on the development of the city. The class which was emphasizing reading used that play for dramatization. In another instance the teacher told the story in a short exciting fashion and let each child choose the part he liked best. Each child then read the section in the chapter pertaining to his favorite selection, and made a cartoon to illustrate it. The cartoons were numbered in large letters and hung around the room. The children read the rest of the chapter to see how many cartoons they could guess correctly and were permitted to use "open book technique" to check their guesses. (The aim was not memorization but reading comprehension and the gaining of concepts.) This whole cartoon sequence took three periods whereas the previously described topic took a minimum of three weeks. The previous topic had the possibility of meeting more needs as the teacher saw them, so the major portion of time was given to such areas.

The earlier experience of using individual books around a common theme is a necessary preliminary to studying a topic in which more structured social studies content is included. When the teachers know the individual abilities of each child, and something of his interests, the search for suitable individual books for each one on, let us say, the Westward Movement, can be intelligently managed. On this subject, a wide range of books does exist. There is *Let the Hurricane Roar*[7] which the teacher can read to the children to give them a feeling that the Westward Movement is about real people, to give them a chance to identify with those people in order to make their study a real-life thing. Such reading also gives the teacher a chance to introduce the concepts he will be teaching and will be asking the children to seek in their own books. There are also such books as *Buffalo Bill* (1948) and *Kit Carson* (1945) by Stevenson, *George Rogers Clark* (1958) by Wilkie, and *Narcissa Whitman* (1957) by Warner, all in the Bobbs-Merrill *Childhood of Famous Americans Series,*[8] and all on about fourth-grade level, some even third, but all of interest at the junior high school level. For those children who may have

[7] R. W. Lane, *Let the Hurricane Roar* (New York: Longmans, Green & Co. 1933).
[8] The Bobbs-Merrill Co., Inc., Indianapolis, Indiana.

reached fifth-grade reading level, there is *Wyatt Earp* by F. Sutton;[9] for those who read below the fourth grade, *Val Rides the Oregon Trail* by Tousey.[10]

Not only does this area of study offer reading materials on all levels, but for all interests. There are adventure books on the Westward Movement for boys; and there are books on real courage and deep responsibility. Boys become men within the covers of one volume, and teen-age boys need this chance to identify. For the girls there are myriads of love stories of the West and as many more portraying human suffering and the role of women in the making of our country. These are only a few areas of typical teen-age interests that can be satisfied; there are numerous others.

Despite these varied reading abilities, despite these varied interests, the situation is manageable and profitable when books being read are used to enrich such concepts as:

> People went West for a number of reasons.
> People of many ethnic backgrounds settled our great West.[11]
> People of courage and perseverance settled the West.

The group discussions can deal with such questions as: Where did the people in your book come from? When did they settle? Does your book say why they chose that particular place? How did the people in your book display courage?—perseverance? How was this similar from book to book? How were these things different? Was everyone courageous? What happened when people did not persevere? In this way the reading in effect becomes "common" even though everyone is reading a different book; it is through such a procedure that each contribution helps to build the larger concept; and it is through this procedure that the larger concept, once gained, helps to give greater meaning to the individual reading materials.

The teacher must also plan ways of learning to use a common social studies textbook properly, for the common textbook need not be disposed of and even has its role to play, especially since it can offer a measure of security both to a young teacher and to children. It must be remembered that the children represent a reading range of about five years. This is not unusual. Even in a gifted class, the range is this great, from grades 10 to 16, for example. But at this upper level no one worries that the common

---

[9] New York, Scholastic Book Services. *(Out of print.)*

[10] Sanford Tousey, *Val Rides the Oregon Trail* (New York: Doubleday & Company, Inc., 1939). *(Out of print.)*

[11] The terminology used here is not necessarily that of the classroom. Concepts are not taught directly, but are the result of many experiences.

textbook is not suitable for all. No one worries because every child can handle it. If it is a textbook on a twelfth-year level and suits only one-third of the class, this is considered good enough. In this sense, the problem is the same. But with children who read below grade level, there are few textbooks simple enough, and few children who can really use them. The important thing teachers need to know is that for children with reading difficulties a common textbook is simply not suitable for independent study. It must be used *with* the teacher under his constant guidance, supervision, and assistance. The teacher cannot assign pages and expect any results. Independent work is done through the individual books which are on their own levels and which they can handle. The common textbook is quite another matter.

In some units which the teachers prepared the common textbook was most successfully introduced after the children had gained some concepts from their reading of individual books, from viewing films, and from short stories on the topic read by the teacher. Many questions arose which the textbook could help answer, thus making the textbook, if not quite a necessity, at least a meaningful source. For example, one child was reading a story which took place in 1845; another was reading about Lewis and Clark, a much earlier date; a third, 1878. Well then, when *was* the Westward Movement? If two squatters claimed the same land, how was it settled? If there were no prisons and no laws, how did they manage the bad men? How did they find their way to the place where they wanted to go? In one book the family was traveling with a covered-wagon train; in another, the family traveled independently. One book said covered-wagon trains were for protection; then how did the single family manage to survive? Questions such as these, which grew out of children's comparing "notes" in class, soon led the teacher and the class to discover that a common textbook is not enough, but that it could help them answer questions which arose when their individual reading was compared. Several different textbooks, at least single copies of them, were necessary so that information not available in one could be sought in another.

In one class where children were making a "movie" of the contents of their chapter,[12] in order to fit their individual books in sequence for the

---

[12] The teacher had handled the reading of the chapter in much the same way as she did a short story. It was a basic reading lesson with the extra motivation of movie-making. The children who could not handle any of the silent reading alone sat with sociometrically chosen classmates who read to them. Another variation to handle individual abilities was provided by the use of a tape recorder into which earphones were plugged so that several children could listen to the chapter at once without disturbing children who could already manage to read the text with minimum assistance.

"talkie part," they found the chapter wholly inadequate in information. The better readers were set to work reading other textbooks to answer the specific questions for which the class still needed answers before they could proceed with their project. The success of this little venture was a surprise and an eye-opener to the teacher who "never in her wildest dreams would ever imagine these children would ask for more books and more content."

PLANNING DAILY LESSONS

In addition to the long-range planning described above, the teacher had to plan daily lessons so all children could learn.

One aspect of structuring lessons which these young teachers had to learn was the importance of varying activities in the course of one session, and the need for focusing these activities in such a way that the lesson remained one lesson rather than three short discrete activities. Activities had to be varied for several reasons: (1) Interest span in activities connected with academic work was still short since the effort that must be put forth was so great, the frustration so powerful and so quick to set in, the feelings of failure so strong, the motivation so lacking. (2) Only through a variety of activities could the teacher discover children's needs and aptitudes; but also only through that same variety could he meet the needs of all the children since each one learned best in a different way. (3) By and large, the children were lacking in many skills already learned by most children and were lacking in experiential background possessed by others. Different skills and wide background of experiences could not be gained through rigid structuring of similar activities.

Let us examine the activities that might be encompassed in one "lesson." Let us suppose that the aim, in addition to enjoying the reading of poems together, was to help children understand their meaning a little more clearly. Teachers were already aware of the values of choral reading of poetry for these children—in particular: (1) Trying out different arrangements of choral reading demands the rereading of a poem many times, and without boredom if the poem is properly chosen for the group. (2) Trying out various arrangements lends itself to discussion focused on immediate performance, but indirectly dealing with the poet's meaning.

The teacher usually introduced a poem by starting a discussion with the children, centered around some aspect of the poem's theme as it bore on the children's experiences. This was relatively easy to do with Eleanor Graham's "SOS" or Ethel Jacobson's "Trick or Treat." Then the teacher read the poem to the children after which their spontaneous reactions to it were discussed very briefly. The teacher had earlier introduced the idea of reading in chorus, and together they tried to work out the first verse. Throughout the whole "working out" process, the teacher encouraged differences of opinion; this gave him an opportunity to lead the children to reread for meaning in order to see which arrangement would suit the meaning better. A boy's voice? A girl's? Solo? Chorus? How do you know? Arrangement after arrangement was tried out to "test" decisions.

Next, each child took his mimeographed copy of the poem and studied the remaining stanzas (or another poem was introduced if the first was too short) and marked on the paper who he thought should say each line. Then the teacher put the children into groups to thrash out their whys and wherefores and to prepare to perform. Each group did perform and the decision of the judges (three of the children had been selected earlier) was final. Sometimes the class was divided in half, each working out a different poem.

Let us see what happened. There were several activities—discussing with the teacher, listening to the poem, reading the poem, making class-wide decisions which required rereading, testing findings, making individual written decisions, holding small-group discussions and practice, and enjoying group performance for the whole class. They talked, they wrote, they listened, they read. Yet all activities were around a central focus and central aim. And the activities commanded enthusiastic and full participation.

The particular variety of activity packed into a lesson or group of lessons depended on the experiences needed by the children which would not only reinforce their skills but aid their comprehension. For example, one series of books concerned immigration to the United States, the struggles of the people who came, the reasons for their coming, the various ways in which their problems were solved. In order to lend a feeling of reality to what they were reading and to aid comprehension, the children were asked to interview someone they knew who had come from another country and to ask certain specific questions. They received some instruction on how to conduct an interview with an adult, and on how to take notes on the interview. This instruction was carried on by means of a role-playing session with the "audience" taking notes. The role-playing incident was followed by a discussion of how the interview was conducted, how it needed to be changed, and also by a discussion of the type of notes children were keeping and how these could be improved. Thus far, the children were talking and listening intently and purposefully, and they were writing. When they returned with their notes of the actual interviews they discussed their findings and wrote up their interviews. From these, a tally was made (in small groups) on what countries people came from, why they came, what problems they encountered. This tally was used for comparisons with ideas in the books they were reading individually.

Now when they read their story books, the content was much more meaningful. Such books as Judson's *Michael's Victory*[13] and *The Lost Violin*[14] could be handled with understanding, whereas without previous experience with the topic this would not have been possible. Many of the words used were familiar as were the complex ideas. *Immigrant, detained, famine* were now familiar friends, as were the ideas of steerage and smuggling and ghettos.

Another area of concern in daily planning was "teaching a skills lesson." Teachers had to learn the fruitlessness of a "skills lesson" without focus on content. Planning for skills teaching had to be done within the context of whatever ideas were being handled. First the principles were established that such lessons should be relatively few for a whole class and that *two* direct aims, content and a skill, for example, were needed. Teachers planned them around common reading materials at first and then helped the children use the newly learned skill in individual ways and with their own reading materials. When a class was discussing and considering the role of the family as educator, one concept the teacher wished to stress was "People have different ideas about how children should be reared." He also wished to teach, as his second aim, the use of context clues to recognize meanings of words. The material which he planned to use for this was "Baby Sitter vs. Ronnie" by Harold Johnson.[15] He planned the opening discussion around the children's experiences as baby sitters and then talked about the title of the story, leading the children to make hypotheses through such questions as, "What do you think the story will be about?" "Do you think Ronnie and the sitter will be on friendly terms?" "What can you guess from the title?" More hypotheses were made by looking at the pictures as the teacher guided with questions: "Is the child friendly?" "What does the sitter seem to be doing about it?"

After the reading, the children's questions or hypotheses were discussed with much going back to the story for defense of ideas they had gleaned. (The four children unable to handle this story at all sat with partners who read to them.) The teacher took time to teach context clues at a point where the children were still interested in the story, writing

---

[13] Clara I. Judson, *Michael's Victory* (Boston: Houghton, Mifflin Co., 1946).
[14] Clara I. Judson, *The Lost Violin* (Boston: Houghton, Mifflin Co., 1947).
[15] In Ruth Strang and Ralph Roberts, *Teen-Age Tales, Book 1* (Boston: D. C. Heath and Co., 1954).

sentences on the board that included words or expressions from the story. For example:

I did such a big favor for Tim's mother but she was not *grateful* at all; she didn't even say thanks.

Children first tried to find clues to the word *grateful* in the sentence. Then, they found the sentence or sentences in which the word was used in the book. They were encouraged to use these context clues as they gave evidence from the book in answer to thought questions planned for further discussion, questions such as, "Do you think Ronnie is clever? Give all the evidence you can." Later, as they read their own books, which the teacher very often gave them time to do or which they did at home, they looked for "What parents seemed to believe about rearing children." They asked their partners[16] about at least one key word and the clues to it for a succession of days until everyone had "caught the idea" and was really using the skill. (This took several weeks.)

Again it must be stressed that only a limited number of such skills needed to be taught to the class as a whole. There were some, of course, which all children needed as in the case of the one cited above. When teachers discovered a universal need, it was more efficient to present the skill to the whole class than to teach it individually, even though it had to be reviewed over and over again individually before all the children had learned to use it for their own purposes.

FINDING SUITABLE MATERIALS

Adequate planning requires a knowledge of materials for children which most teachers first starting out do not have. It means browsing through libraries and through published reading lists for materials that are suitable.[17] Only recent lists should be used since books go out of print so quickly.

[16] It will be recalled that a short time was given daily for partners to read to each other.

[17] Some suggestions for aids to finding such books are: G. D. Spache, *Good Reading for Poor Readers* (Reading Laboratory and Clinic, University of Florida, Gainesville, Florida); Anita E. Dunn, Mabel E. Jackman, Bernice C. Bush, *Fare for the Reluctant Reader* (Albany, New York: Capital Area School Development Association, State University of New York, New York State College for Teachers, 1952); Ruth Strang, *Gateways to Readable Books* (New York: H. W. Wilson and Company, 1952); and *Bulletin of the Center for Children's Books* (University of Chicago, Graduate Library School), a monthly bulletin to the subscriber.

Teachers must use all lists with care. Often, books are assigned a lower reading level than is actually the case when one uses them with a child. For example, books rated as grade 3 are sometimes found to be impossible for a reader scoring grade 3 on a group test.

Teachers should study carefully the earlier reading test scores of the children and then peruse many books on various levels to "get a sense" of what each level means, in format, vocabulary, number of new words introduced and repetition, length of sentence, and content ideas.

Lack of familiarity with suitable materials can be and often was a very serious obstacle to the success of a venture such as described in this pamphlet. When several suggestions were offered to one teacher for introducing a unit, he was most intrigued by the process of reading a short story to the children, holding a discussion, and beginning a list of questions or problems raised by them. This whole process is not "simple." The teacher never got further than selecting and reading part of the story. He had chosen "Heroine of the Plains" from a reader that he happened to find in the school. It was a diary-like account, not suitable for oral reading, and uninteresting even to an adult. He complained, "The reading didn't go over. The children weren't interested." For such teachers, then, there is the whole process of learning what will "go" with the children.

Another teacher insisted on American folklore and the "imaginative literature" because his children "had no imagination" and he was intent on developing it. This was a "need" as important as any other, in his opinion. No one attempted to persuade him otherwise. Before the end of the third day he sought a sympathetic and helpful ear: He had "lost" his class, they weren't interested, they were "fighting" him, he had "given up." Other teachers with whom he was planning his work helped him to analyze the situation. It was a "need," but whose? Did the children feel it as a need? What was the evidence? Was there a hierarchy of needs? Was it possible that some developmental tasks were so much more important to children at this time that the need to develop imagination simply was not next in line? Was it true that all children rejected Paul Bunyan? Was it possible to help those children who were ready for him to enjoy him now? This teacher knew that folklore was at that time being more than just "accepted" in another group. What was the second teacher doing that might be helpful? Those children had interviewed parents for "hand-me-down stories," had tallied the possible places of origin, had seen the similarities and differences, had noted basic ideas in them, and were now reading folk-tales from around the world "to see if even in China and South America children heard such stories."

As time went on and teachers realized the importance of finding suitable materials they began to share the books they discovered with other teachers and even planned to share the burden of reading a number of them. They kept a card file for their information to help in planning. Each card showed the approximate reading level of the book and the interest level, the number of pages in it, the unit areas to which it would make a contribution, the specific concepts emphasized in it, and three or four specific page references of sections suitable for reading aloud or for use in introducing the book or for materials constituting a vicarious experience. This method proved invaluable as a timesaver and as an aid to long-range planning.

If the teacher began the first year with a room collection of at least thirty individual books, those children not motivated to find their own could select from these. Paperbacks were a popular source of reading material. Teachers themselves purchased such books as *Old Yeller*[18] and *Mama's Bank Account*[19] in order to have something on the shelves when school began. Later, a most helpful source was the Arrow Book Club (Scholastic Book Services) which features books at fourth- to sixth-grade reading levels for less than twenty-five cents a copy. It took a little while, however, for teachers to organize themselves and to learn the possibilities of using such materials. Books from the Arrow Book Club that were popular with the children were *Henry Huggins, Eddie's Pay Dirt, On Your Toes, Susie!, Deadline at Spook Cabin, Ghostly Trio, Arrow Book of Ghost Stories, Chimp in the Family, Afraid to Ride, Kit Carson, Father's Big Improvements,* and *Ben-Hur* (adapted by Willis Lindquist). These books were passed from one to the other until they were literally worn out. When teachers had books like these on the classroom shelves right at the beginning of the year, many problems of motivation (plus the added "strain" of children resisting trips to the library because they really did not want to read) were eliminated. Because they were available, handy, easy to carry, light weight, "skinny," and within the interest and ability range of many of the children they were read.

Another indispensable source of materials was the *American Adventure Series*[20] including such titles as *Squanto and the Pilgrims, Buffalo Bill,* and *The Rush for Gold.* Children enjoy these because the format is excellent and the content challenging to a teen-ager, while the reading level of the series of about seventeen books ranges from grade two to six. Still another source was the Garrard Press series called *Discovery Books.* This includes such books as Clara Barton's *Soldier of Mercy* and Theodore Roosevelt's *Man of Action.* They are on a second- to fourth-grade reading level but have high interest level. Some of the *Beginner Books,* distributed by Random House, were a boon for the teacher because they could be given to the child immediately on entry into the junior high

[18] Fred Gipson, *Old Yeller* (New York: Pocket Books, Inc., 1957).
[19] Kathryn Forbes, *Mama's Bank Account* (New York: Bantam Books, 1947).
[20] *American Adventure Series,* published by Harper & Row, New York.

school and were accepted by the child who was virtually a nonreader. There is Bennett Cerf's *Book of Riddles* which children poured over for a long stretch of time, and also his *Book of Laughs*. Garrard Press's *Junior Science Books Series* is on a primary grade level. The *Book of Beavers* held some children spellbound and offered them so much satisfaction that it was voluntarily reread. Not to be overlooked is the earlier-mentioned *Childhood of Famous Americans Series*.

The importance of good room libraries cannot be overestimated.[21] They must be adequate in size and they must be geared to the interest and abilities of the children who occupy the room. Each year teachers add a substantial number to their collection, mostly from paperback issues. Each year there are new needs to be met and again teachers are on the search for new materials. Even the five-and-dime stores yield books which no other source can supply.

The greatest reward for teachers who have made an effort to know the children, who have made intelligent curriculum adjustments, who have prepared daily lessons and made long-range plans so that every child can learn, who have taken time to become familiar with children's materials, is that all of this planting bears its hoped-for-fruit.

[21]This is especially so in schools where children are permitted to check out books from the school library for two days only. Some children cannot read a book in two days!

4 • The Evidence

EVIDENCES OF GROWTH OR LACK OF IT CAN BE OF MANY TYPES, DEPEND-
ing on the aims of teaching. Some types of evidence are relatively simple
to gather, others quite complex because of the nature of the goals, the
"instruments" available, and the complexity of influences in a child's life.
It is a simple matter to administer a standardized test and find a score in
reading; it is not difficult to keep a record of all books each child reads.
But it is another matter to find tools for measuring what happens to children psychologically as a result of the experiences they have in school.

Our chief aim in gathering evidence of children's progress in this
project was to appraise our own efforts, to evaluate the extent to which
we were meeting our complex goals, and thus to provide guides for our-
selves as we moved along toward the attainment of those goals. Data-
gathering could not be confined to one particular point in time. It was
necessary to gather it continuously; in fact this process was unavoidable.
For example, in the midst of a class session in which the teacher was introducing some exciting books to be read in connection with a new unit,
a child called out, "You know, last year I tried to read that book and I
just couldn't make it out. I'm reading it now and it's wonderful! I hate to
put it down when my mother calls me for supper. It's a corker." On another occasion, as the teacher moved about the room listening to partners
as they read to each other, he heard a child say "save" instead of "slave,"
and in the next sentence "heard" for "headed" and "started" for "stared."
Such bits of information gathered daily by the alert teacher told him much
about the progress of individual children, about what the next steps must
be in planning for the growth of those who were already readers, of those
who miscalled words yet managed to get the meaning of the passage, and
of those who knew the words but failed to "make any sense" out of them.
Each day the teachers managed through one activity or another to discover something new about a number of children. These discoveries provided clues to progress and to future goals and plans.

We were also concerned with the intangibles which cannot (at this stage in our knowledge about test development) be measured with tests: The truly professional attitude which young teachers developed, the deep regard they showed for the welfare of the children, the way in which the children's behavior took on a positive note as they strove toward maturity, the liking for reading which they developed, the measure of self-confidence which they gained, their attitudes about learning and school work in general—these and many other things we knew to be of great importance.

USE OF STANDARDIZED TESTS

However, we felt also the obligation to examine more formally the reading progress of the children, and therefore we planned a simple testing "program," not only as a guide to future planning but as an evaluation of achievement. A summary of the test results of one class will serve as evidence of progress over a period of one year and a half—the period that spans the beginning of grade seven to the half-way point in grade eight.

By May of the seventh year, the average reading *growth* for the class in one year[1] was only 0.6, as measured by the Metropolitan Achievement Intermediate Test. A second battery of reading tests was administered in January of the eighth year, and in the six school months between May and January, the average reading growth was 2.5 years, measuring paragraph meaning only. This improvement was well above expectations. Ten children made three years of improvement or more in that six months, eight made at least two years, two made one year, and one made six months. As will be explained later, some of these scores for individual children demonstrated growth that was not statistically significant.

It would appear that there were several factors contributing to the differences in results between the two periods of time—the seventh grade up to May, and the eighth grade up to January: (1) The teacher was new and in the process of being assisted, and was learning new procedures. By the time the children reached eighth grade, she already had some skills in building a program and in carrying it through. (2) The first year in the junior high school is an adjustment year for the children who need time to grow. This may be the year in which they absorb much with the results of that absorption not apparent, as far as is evident from standardized tests, until the next year. (3) Many of these children entered the seventh grade convinced that they were incapable of learning to read well, of

[1] The children had been tested in grade six, before entering this school.

"making the grade." They had had years of struggle with reading which had sapped their confidence in themselves. It takes time for a teacher to build confidence lost over the years; it is not something that can be done in a month or two. (4) They remained with the same teacher that year; they now had confidence in her ability to help them; it was she who built their self-confidence. The teacher, in turn, knew the children better, sensed their moods and reactions more quickly, and could utilize her knowledge in terms of grouping and giving individual help more efficiently.

It must not be forgotten that there were *thirty* children enrolled in this class, with many kinds of psychological problems already quite apparent. (Data were collected on only twenty-nine because one girl, who had a serious emotional problem, left after the seventh year.) It must be remembered, too, that these children entered with reading grades (based on test scores) ranging from 2.6 to 5.1. The average grade was 4.1 but eleven children were reading on a third-grade level or below. Assuming the IQ scores are correct, the expectation is that the children cannot make a year's growth in a year's time. These same children made two and one-half years' growth in six months. Is the IQ score accurate? That question arose immediately. The results as measured by a verbal test (Pintner) in the sixth grade showed a range of 67 to 106 with the mean of 87.9. In grade seven, an SRA nonverbal was administered, and here the range was from 68 to 125 with the mean at 105.0. As mentioned earlier, the purpose in administering the SRA was to help the teachers accept the children, to encourage them to encourage the children in the belief that they really could learn.

Later, when we tried to study the relationship between the Pintner and the SRA we discovered the rank-difference coefficient of correlation to be +.23. A variety of comparisons were made of SRA results with reading improvement, and Pintner results with reading improvement, but no definite relationships emerged. It is important to stress the fallibility of test results—both IQ and reading. It is important, particularly now when school systems seem to be using reading scores as a priority factor in nonpromotion.

We know that when children cannot read, this inability affects the IQ score. But another question, then, needs to be asked. If their IQ's are higher than tested, why didn't they learn to read before this? One can hazard a guess that the gain was not made in six months even though test results showed this to be so. In other words, something probably was "perking" in those first months which did not become apparent until later. It may be theorized that children's negative feelings about themselves in those early months prevented efficient learning, and also that the teachers' insecurity about what *they* were able to do was another factor.

One of the problems teachers found difficult to face was the fact that an obtained grade score could mean something quite different from what it seemed to indicate. Although teachers could accept the fact that an "obtained" score and the child's "true" score could be two quite different things, it was still difficult for them to "really believe" it and to act on it. A retest was given in one class within three or four weeks of a previous test because of a mix-up in the level of the test given. On this second test, the scores of many children were quite different from their scores on the earlier test. Some children "went down," a particularly alarming "fact" to teachers. What could have happened? Why was this so? It was then that it became possible to help teachers acquire a deeper understanding of the difference between a score on only one test and a child's "true" score. It was then that teachers could see how misleading one test score could be, how important it was to interpret scores properly. They examined the manual which accompanies those tests in order to see the authors' interpretation of its reliability and validity. They discussed the populations from which the norms for the two tests had been obtained, and compared these with their own children. They began to understand that test scores for one child are less reliable than test scores for whole groups of children. The word "began" is used advisedly. There was still some learning to be done. It was difficult for the teachers to realize that the same grade score or a lower grade score over a given period of time does not necessarily indicate lack of progress. It might merely be indicative of the fact that a particular child was making *gains* at a slower rate than the population with which the test was standardized, and that children whose grade scores in a year and a half went from 4.2 to 9.8, for example, might be making gains at a much faster rate than the population with which the test was standardized.

Once teachers began to work intensively on reading problems, they became more concerned about the *differences* between two test scores of any given child than they were about any one of his scores. This was a "natural" phenomenon, because they were interested in every shred of evidence of growth or of lack of growth. We found that manuals of various test makers differed in the information they gave about reliability. For example, the manual for the *Gates Basic Reading Tests* gives the degree of reliability for the difference between reading grades on two tests. A child who scores anywhere from 3.0 to 4.9 must show a difference of one whole year (1.0) before the difference can be considered reliable. A child who scores between 5.0 and 6.9 must show a difference of at least

1.6, and a child who scores from 9.0 to 12.9 must show a difference of 2.6. This requirement is due to the fact that the *difference* between two scores is *less* reliable than either one of the two scores. Thus, if a child received a reading grade of 5.0 on one test in the series, and 5.4 in the second test, the difference of 0.4 would be considered neither reliable nor practically significant.[2]

One of the most fruitful activities which helped teachers understand the differences in test scores was a brief attempt at item-analysis. We compared a few items on one test with a few on the other. What abilities did the teachers think they were measuring? Could it be that they were measuring different kinds of reading ability? Were these abilities the same as those being stressed in our program?

We also looked at other conditions which can affect test scores. Was one test given in the morning on a Monday and the other on a Friday in the afternoon? What was going on in school that day? A soccer game? Who administered the test? The same teacher? What interruptions occurred? And what test conditions existed which were of a personal nature? Did the child leave home that morning without eating breakfast, and after having a quarrel with his mother? Was this the day he returned after a four-day absence from school because his face had been badly cut in a street fight?

Such were some of the questions we knew had to be answered before we could say a particular child read at the 4.5 grade level. Rather, teachers learned to think in terms of "She *tested* 4.5 on the Metropolitan that particular day."

Another understanding that came as a result of testing and studying the children's responses was that an eighth-grader who scored on the test at the fourth-year level handled the reading situation in quite another way from a fourth-grader. In the first place, he tended to approach the testing situation with the intense anxiety an adolescent feels about failure after he has met years of it. In the second place, he tended to react differently to particular test items. Those which were more "interesting" to him, with respect to content, received a more careful response, and therefore he managed to score positively on these items. Those that "looked dull," he simply skipped or "marked any old way," as he went through the test.

[2] The Metropolitan Test makers give standard error and probable error based on standard scores rather than on grade scores. However, in consultation with Harcourt, Brace and World, Inc. (New York), it was discovered that for the 1959 tests, the standard error in terms of grade equivalents for children near grade 4.0 is .4. (See G. H. Hildreth, *Metropolitan Achievement Tests Manual for Interpreting* (New York: Harcourt, Brace & World, Inc.. 1948), page 9.

VOLUME OF READING

Another piece of evidence lies in the amount of reading the children did on their own levels. The sheer number of books some children managed to digest was impressive. Although keeping a record of children's reading is a relatively easy thing to do, not all teachers nor all children found this assignment appealing. Nor did teachers at first see the importance of accurate records for purposes of evaluation. Therefore, we kept close reading records only in the second semester of the seventh grade. Before this, the children were still reading relatively little, and most erratically. By the second semester, the teachers' efforts at motivating reading had taken effect and children began to understand what books were suitable for them, so that they were not so tenacious about holding on to George Orwell's *Animal Farm* for a month or six weeks simply because they had discovered what they thought was a "dog or horse story."

In this second semester the children read from four to eleven books, not counting the books they had read for the younger-sibling project which was officially completed by now, but which many children continued for personal reasons.[3] Neither did this count include the common readings in class of plays, poetry, and short stories. Their reading was mainly of an order typified for the boys by *Homer Price, Henry Huggins, Circus Boy, Bat Boy of the Giants, Trouble after School, Lou Gehrig, Gene Autry, Roy Rogers,* and *Trouble at Beaver Dam.* But even by this time there was one boy who read *Old Yeller,* another who read *The Red Pony,*[4] *Smoky, the Cow Horse,*[5] and *Tom Sawyer.* The girls' reading was typified by *The Ringmaster's Secret, Heidi, Five Little Peppers, Happy Hollisters, Sue Barton—Student Nurse, Black Beauty, The Big Wave, The Great Airport Mystery, Lonesome Boy, That Boy Johnny, The Strange Echo, Mystery in Old Quebec, Annie Oakley, The Six-Fingered Glove Mystery, In the Sunken Garden,* and *Love Is Beautiful.* One girl had read *Little Women,* two had read *Tom Sawyer* and *Junior Miss,* and one had read *Old Yeller.* These books are cited here to give an idea of what the children chose when encouraged to make their own selections. It must be remembered, of course, that availability has much to do with what is chosen.

Certainly of equal importance with sheer numbers of books con-

---

[3] Each teacher tried some variation of the project in which children read to younger ones.

[4] By John Steinbeck (New York: Bantam Books, 1955).

[5] By William James (New York: Charles Scribner's Sons, 1929).

sumed was the factor of "fit" to level and taste. Children wrote reactions to the books they read—brief and simple "reports" which indicated their *enjoyment* of books. Only on occasion were detailed reports called for. We kept down the volume of report writing so that it would not become a chore. We feared that too many reports would kill budding reading interests. There were plenty of occasions for writing about books and talking about them, but rarely for "reporting." Simple reactions were written by children in some classrooms for the card file, in others for a mimeographed sheet. One boy wrote about *Tom Sawyer:* "I thought the book was very good. I would go out to buy that book, I like it so much." Another wrote about *Roll the Red Wagon:* "My friends would like this book because it is exciting and terrific," and yet another said about *Roy Rogers:* "The book was very good. I could read it in about five hours. It wasn't a hard book that would take you about seven hours. I enjoyed the book a lot." It is interesting to note that these were the boys who showed very great reading growth—4.0, 3.0, and 3.1 years respectively.

CHILDREN'S FEELINGS ABOUT THEMSELVES AS LEARNERS

Another method of judging the growth of children is by studying the way they feel about what they have learned. During the last week of school in their seventh grade, they were asked to write, among other things, on the topic "What I Feel I Gained in the Seventh Grade." They could have mentioned anything at all—height, weight, social graces, anything. But most of them did not. By far, the greatest number of children mentioned reading. Of course, they knew their core teacher was concentrating on reading and it was their core teacher who asked them to write on this topic, but they were specifically told that any area they felt important would be acceptable. Following are a few very enlightening excerpts which have a ring of sincerity. They show that the children have learned the importance of *reading* in order to learn to read, and they reveal some of the children's problems and reactions to experiences:

GIRL: I think since I came to this school, I've went up in everything. I mostly went up in reading. In my other school I was very poor in reading. I'm so surprise to see how well I'm reading now. . . . Last year I didn't read as much as I do now. . . . I changed altogether since I came to this school. I never enjoyed reading as much as I do now. I used to go to the Library and get a book and I would never read it. Now I get lots of books and I read them and enjoy them.

GIRL: At the beginning of the year I didn't like to read. Last year I never read because me and three other kids never read with the teacher. The teacher never liked to read with us.

GIRL: When I came to this school I couldn't read. I think I was one of the worst readers in the whole school. I just couldn't pick up a book and read. I just wasn't interested. Then when you started with reading and made us pick up a book and read I had no choice so I started with a book I had home which I tried to read before but wasn't interested in. It was called *Kay Tracy in the Sunken Garden*. After I started it I got more and more interested till I loved to read. Every time I went home I didn't do anything but read till I read two or three books a week. That's how I learned to read.

BOY: Reading keeps me out of trouble. That's the good part of it all. Reading made me sick. Now it seems fun to me. Reading is getting better and better when I read now.

BOY: I have learned many things this year but I think I improved most of all in reading. I did not like to read at all when I came here but now I really like to read. I think that you should use this system with your next class too.

But one boy, despite his growth in reading, had some negative reactions to at least one procedure: "I do not think your system was too good, because I found out when you read to yourself you read much better. . . . When you are reading to a teacher you are scared, I know I am when I read to you."

Another bit of evidence that children *were* reading came from parents. They expressed surprise and delight that a child on occasion voluntarily read "something funny" to his mother while she prepared dinner, and they were astonished that the children sat down with books without being forced to do so by the parents. Parents of the children who made obvious improvement had much to say about a number of things ranging from "He cares about the way he looks and dresses; he even combs his hair more now," to "He behaves so much better than he used to," and "He always reads to his little sister now—takes more time with her," or "He reads the *Long Island Press* every night now. He never used to be interested in a newspaper." One parent said, "He asked us to subscribe to the *Reader's Digest* for him. So we did," and another remarked, "He reads every night before going to sleep; we have to fight to get him to put out the light." One mother was particularly proud because "He takes science books out of the library," and another was happy because "His attitude toward school has changed; he actually likes to go."

TEACHERS' INFORMAL ESTIMATES OF
CHILDREN'S GROWTH

Even before the conclusion of the seventh year, the teachers were able to see some remarkable changes in the children which were harbingers of the changes that later were measurable on test scores. They estimated that one-half of their children were what they would call "readers," children who now had "the reading habit." They noted such positive progress as, "He seems to know how to go about finding out what he doesn't know. For instance, when he couldn't recognize 'clear', he turned back the page in the story until he found a *cl* word, all by himself—I just watched him do it—and he found 'clap'. Then he turned back and first he said 'clar', but then he read ahead when he realized that wasn't a word, and from the context he figured out 'clear'. I thought that was pretty good. He did all this without my giving him one word of direction."

About one child a teacher commented, "I don't know whether I'd call him a reader or not. He has developed the reading habit in only a limited sense. He will read only books about war; any other type of book will not hold his interest." The teacher was aware, however, that even this represented significant growth. To be called a reader in one area is a far cry from being a nonreader. There was a limited number of children who made such amazing progress that the teacher commented about one, for example, "A voracious reader! This has developed only during this term. I can tell by his attitude toward reading at the beginning of the term— which was a negative one."

No teacher reported at the end of the seventh year having a child who "didn't care." Children who previously refused to ask for specific help now did so willingly as they lost their fear of being considered stupid and as they became aware of the specific weaknesses which were theirs. At first they were aware only that they did not know how to read. Now they knew tangible factors which represented weaknesses. They knew, when they read "falling" for "failing" and "it didn't quite make sense," that they "hadn't noticed details in the middle of the word." But when they could not unravel the word from the context even after they had "looked carefully" and had read ahead, they decided that it was a question of vocabulary, a word whose meaning they did not know, and that at this point they needed to seek aid.

There was one great weakness which teachers were not able to overcome, especially in the three or four boys who had shown little progress by the end of the seventh grade. These boys were the ones who still refused to give up their strangle hold on books far too difficult for them. Teachers knew there was a psychological reason for this, and that probably these were children who had not yet been "reached."

Teachers noticed a marked decrease among the children in "laughing at each other for stupid mistakes," and a tangible increase in the degree of self-assurance with which children tackled learning problems connected with reading. Children who had once retired from the struggle easily were now pitching in and refusing to give up.

We feel sure these results were obtained, not because of one isolated thing that was done, but because of a multifaceted program. This program included assistance to teachers, special periods for teachers to plan together and to talk over problems, concentration on the mental health of the children, planning an integrated language arts program for the children, giving the children sufficient time with one teacher who was herself receiving support from administrators and consultants, using certain sound procedures in the classroom, and building a whole school in which such things not only could happen, but were bound to happen, a school in which there was a total commitment on the part of teachers and administrators—and college people who worked with them—to make this a place in which the living and the learning that went on would continue to become better and richer.